United States Presidents

Abraham Lincoln

Karen Judson

Enslow Publishers, Inc.

44 Fadem Road   PO Box 38
Box 699   Aldershot
Springfield, NJ 07081 Hants GU12 6BP
USA   UK

Copyright © 1998 by Karen Judson

Library of Congress Cataloging–in–Publication Data

Judson, Karen, 1941–
    Abraham Lincoln / Karen Judson.
        p. cm — (United States Presidents)
    Includes bibliographical references (p. 116) and index.
    Summary: Traces the life of the sixteenth president from his
    humble childhood in Kentucky through his years as a businessman,
    lawyer, and state legislator, to his role in preserving the Union
    during the Civil War.
    ISBN 0–89490–939–8
    1. Lincoln, Abraham, 1809–1865—Juvenile literature.
    2. Presidents—United States—Biography—Juvenile literature.
    [1. Lincoln, Abraham, 1809–1865. 2. Presidents.] I. Title.
    II. Series.
    E457.905.J8   1998
    973.7'092
    [B]—DC21   97–23025
                                                    CIP
                                                     AC

Printed in the United States of America

10 9 8 7 6 5 4 3 2 1

Illustration Credits: Joan L. Chaconas, p. 84; © Corel
Corporation, p. 106; Library of Congress, pp. 22, 39, 53, 55, 65, 76,
77, 86, 100; The Lincoln Museum, pp. 4, 11, 46, 80, 82, 94, 110;
Surratt House Museum, pp. 73, 91, 93, 104.

Source Document Credits: Library of Congress, pp. 19, 49, 57,
66, 70, 72, 74, 88, 90; Karen Judson, p. 68.

Cover Illustration: White House Historical Association

Contents

One of the most familiar photographs of Abraham Lincoln, taken February 9, 1864. This profile was used as a guide in the making of the Lincoln penny.

1

SNEAKING INTO WASHINGTON

A t 10:00 P.M. on February 22, 1861, a special train from Harrisburg, Pennsylvania, pulled into west Philadelphia. Three men slipped quietly from the train's single car. The tallest of the three men wore a long overcoat and a felt hat pulled down over his brow. The men walked quickly across the tracks to catch the midnight train to Baltimore, Maryland.

Two of the men helped the third man board the waiting train. The two helpers were railroad detective Allan Pinkerton and an armed bodyguard named Ward Hill Lamon. The tall man was taken through a rear door of the train, into a private sleeping cabin. Here he removed his coat and hat and crawled into a cramped bunk.

The train with its hidden passenger pulled out of the station. If all went well, it would arrive in Baltimore around 3:00 A.M.

At 3:15 A.M. the train pulled into the Calvert Street Station in Baltimore. From there the tall man who had boarded the train in secret was rushed across town to catch the Baltimore & Ohio train for Washington, D.C. The mystery passenger changed trains without being seen. His train arrived in the nation's capital about two and a half hours later.

It was early in the morning on February 23 when the night train from Baltimore pulled into Washington, D.C. The man who had ridden in secret then left the train and rode away in a horse-drawn carriage. He was taken to Willard's Hotel at Fourteenth Street and Pennsylvania Avenue.

The man who traveled in the dead of night to reach Washington, D.C., that February morning was Abraham Lincoln. On November 6, 1860, about two months before his secret arrival in the nation's capital, Lincoln had been elected the sixteenth president of the United States.

Why did the newly elected president sneak into Washington, instead of arriving in the usual way? Because Lincoln was unpopular with many Americans and had received many death threats. He had won enough electoral votes to be elected—180 out of a possible 300—but he had received just 39 percent of the popular vote. Electors in fifteen states did not vote for him. In ten states not one voter checked his name on the ballot.[1]

Because he was against slavery, Lincoln was not popular in the Southern states where slave-holding was legal. He was also unpopular with some Northerners, who feared he would push the South into leaving the Union. If this happened, the North's profitable trade with the South would end. Lincoln had vowed to preserve the Union at all costs, and many Americans feared this would lead to civil war.

When Lincoln was elected in 1860, America was in turmoil. Opinions were hotly divided over slavery and states' rights. Some people believed each state's rights were more important than the rights of the federal government. Many Northerners and Southerners wanted to see the end of slavery. They were called abolitionists. Some abolitionists protested peaceably. Others were violent, beating and killing those who opposed them.

Southerners who did not want to see slavery end believed their way of life depended on slave labor. They thought Lincoln would not care about their interests if he was elected president. These Southerners voted to secede, or withdraw, from the Union and set up their own government.

The South had long threatened secession. When Andrew Jackson was president (1829–1837), South Carolina threatened to secede over high tariffs. In December 1832, Jackson issued a proclamation, or statement, to the people of South Carolina, explaining that under the United States Constitution, secession was illegal. He said he would use military force if any state should try to secede. When tariffs were lowered, South Carolina no longer threatened to leave the Union. Jackson predicted, however, that the South would eventually "blow up a storm on the slave question."[2]

The slavery and states' rights questions continued to fester. When Lincoln was elected president, some Southern states were again threatening to secede.

By early February 1861, South Carolina had seceded from the Union and six more Southern states soon followed: Mississippi, Florida, Alabama, Georgia, Louisiana, and Texas.[3] These states formed a separate government called the Confederate States of America, or the Confederacy.

On February 18, 1861, the provisional Congress of the Confederate States made Jefferson Davis provisional president of the Confederacy. That same year Southern voters elected him to a six-year term in office. (Davis was a United States senator from Mississippi who resigned from Congress when his state seceded.) He was inaugurated on February 22, 1862, in Richmond, Virginia, the capital of the Confederacy.[4]

After the November 1861 election, President-elect Lincoln decided to travel to Washington, D.C., by train. The trip would be a grand journey, allowing the new president to speak to the people as his train wound through the North.

Lincoln left his home in Springfield, Illinois, on

February 12, 1861, and reached Washington, D.C., eleven days later. The train stopped at Indianapolis, Indiana; Cincinnati and Columbus, Ohio; and Pittsburgh, Pennsylvania. From Pittsburgh it backtracked to Cleveland, Ohio, then it went on to Buffalo and Albany, New York. It traveled south along the Hudson River to New York City and on down to Harrisburg and Philadelphia, Pennsylvania; to Baltimore, Maryland; and finally, to Washington, D.C.

Celebrations in honor of the president were held all along the train's route. On some days he delivered as many as twelve speeches. President Lincoln's right hand was swollen and sore by the time the trip was over, from shaking thousands of hands at each stop.

Lincoln's wife, Mary, and their three sons, Robert, seventeen; Willie, eleven; and Thomas "Tad," eight, joined him on the train in Indianapolis, where Mary had been shopping. Also with the Lincolns on the train were several friends, Ward Hill Lamon acting as bodyguard, secretaries John G. Nicolay and John Milton Hay, campaign manager Judge David Davis, four army guards, and Lincoln's hired African-American servant and friend, William A. Johnson.

On February 21, when his train reached Philadelphia, Lincoln heard that there was a plot to kill him when he changed trains in Baltimore. Detective Allan Pinkerton had been on duty in Baltimore for several days, and he reported much anti-Lincoln talk in that city. Moreover, the police chief there did not like Lincoln and could not be trusted to protect him.[5] Lincoln would be vulnerable in Baltimore because he had to travel across town to change trains. He was urged to cancel his speeches in Philadelphia and in Harrisburg and head straight for Washington, D.C. Lincoln refused, but finally agreed to be taken through Baltimore in secret.

Thus Abraham Lincoln, who was to become one of the most respected American presidents, arrived secretly in the nation's capital to take office. When the press and people finally heard about Lincoln sneaking into Washington, D.C., they made fun of him. "We take it for granted that Mr. Lincoln is not wanting in personal courage," stated a sarcastic editorial in the *New York Tribune*.[6]

Embarrassed by the incident, Lincoln later said he regretted it. "I did not then, nor do I now believe I should have been assassinated had I gone through Baltimore as first contemplated," he told Illinois Congressman Isaac N. Arnold. "But I thought it wise to run no risk where no risk was necessary."[7]

Lincoln knew that he would have a hard job as president. Southern members of Congress were bound to oppose this man who wanted to end slavery and who had said he would preserve the Union at all costs. Furthermore, if the North and the South went to war against each other, he could be forever blamed by both sides for having caused a civil war.

Still, President Lincoln took office, hopeful that the country's problems could be solved. His speech at

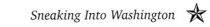

Some newspapers made fun of Lincoln's stealthy trip from Harrisburg, Pennsylvania, to Washington, D.C., on February 23, 1861. This cartoon shows him disguised in a Scottish kilt and tam (a woolen hat).

Independence Hall in Philadelphia on February 22, 1861, told of his faith in the Declaration of Independence. (At the end, it also hinted at his knowledge of the Baltimore plot to kill him.)

> I have never had a feeling politically that did not spring from the . . . Declaration of Independence. I have often inquired of myself, what great principle or idea it was that kept this Confederacy so long together. It was not the mere matter of the separation of the colonies from the mother land; but something in that Declaration giving liberty, not alone to the people of this country, but hope to the world for all future time. It was that which gave promise that in due time the weights should be lifted from the shoulders of all men, and that all should have an equal chance. . . . If this country cannot be saved without giving up that principle—I was about to say I would rather be assassinated on this spot than to surrender it.[8]

Perhaps because he knew his job as president would be difficult and dangerous, on the day Lincoln left Springfield for Washington, D.C., he already seemed to be looking forward to the return trip. When his law partner, William H. Herndon, asked him what to do with the sign that hung outside their law office, Lincoln replied, "Let it hang there undisturbed. Give our clients to understand that the election of a president makes no difference in the firm. If I live, I'm coming back some time, and then we'll go right on practicing as if nothing had happened."[9] At that, he left the building and the city, never to return.

2

BORN IN A LOG CABIN

In 1776, the same year that the Declaration of Independence was written, a farmer named Abraham Lincoln lived in Rockingham County, Virginia. He farmed 210 acres left to him by his father, John Lincoln, one of the many European settlers in the Shenandoah Valley.

This Abraham Lincoln and his wife, Bathsheba, had three sons and two daughters. The sons were named Mordecai, Josiah, and Thomas. The Lincoln daughters were Mary and Nancy. In 1782, Lincoln moved his wife and five children to Kentucky. Here he filed claims for more than five thousand acres of Kentucky farmland.

The Lincolns were becoming wealthy landowners when tragedy struck. In 1786, Lincoln was killed by an American Indian while he was working in a field. His three sons were with him but managed to run away. As was customary at that time, Abraham Lincoln's estate passed to his oldest son, Mordecai. Josiah and Thomas were left on their own in the world.

As he grew, Thomas Lincoln worked at any job he could find. He farmed, built houses and dams, made cabinets, cut wood, and guarded prisoners in a local jail. In 1806, at the age of twenty-eight, while living in Elizabethtown, Kentucky, he met and married twenty-three-year-old Nancy Hanks.

The couple lived in various cabins near whatever job Lincoln had at the time. Then in 1808, he built a log cabin on three hundred acres of land that he had bought for two hundred dollars. The one-room cabin at their Sinking Spring Farm had one door, one window, a chimney, and a dirt floor. Here, about three miles from Hodgensville, Kentucky, Abraham Lincoln, the future president of the United States, was born, on February 12, 1809. The baby was named after his grandfather Abraham.

Thomas and Nancy Lincoln had three children. Sarah was born two years before Abraham, in 1807, and Thomas, Jr., was born a year after Abraham, in 1810. The infant, Thomas, Jr., lived only a few days.

When Abraham was two and Sarah was four, the Lincolns moved to a new farm, on the Cumberland Trail. The land here proved too poor to farm, so Thomas Lincoln bought a smaller, more fertile farm ten miles away, near Knob Creek in Kentucky.

Abraham Lincoln was seven when his family moved again. In 1816, the Lincolns started a new household across the Ohio River in the Indiana wilderness. Abraham's father left Kentucky because at that time clear land titles were difficult to get. Also, as members of the Separate Baptist Church, Thomas and Nancy Lincoln opposed slavery, and Kentucky was a slave state.

Thomas Lincoln believed no person should be slave to another. Because he had competed with slaves for jobs for most of his adult life, he also believed slavery gave the slaveholders an unfair advantage over poor white laborers. Why pay workers when slaves could do the same job?

Abraham Lincoln grew up sharing his parents' views on slavery. In 1864, he told a Kentucky newspaper editor that he was "naturally anti-slavery. If slavery is not wrong," he added, "nothing is wrong. I can not remember when I did not so think, and feel."[1]

Some historians have said that Lincoln also hated slavery because as a boy he worked like a slave. He worked on the family farm and for neighbors, giving every penny he earned to his father.[2]

Friends of young Abraham Lincoln called him Abe. They said that he was hardworking and honest, like his father. He was also curious, like his mother. He liked to tell funny stories and was lively and outgoing most of the time. Nevertheless, sometimes he seemed sad and went off by himself.

Thomas and his family cleared and planted the land

on their Indiana farm. Soon they had saved enough money to buy more land. Then their luck turned.

In 1818, when Abe was nine years old and Sarah was eleven, their mother, Nancy, fell ill. Within a week, she died from an illness people on the frontier called milk sickness. It was caused by drinking the milk of cows that had eaten the poisonous white snakeroot plant. After Nancy's death, her nephew, Dennis Hanks, eighteen, moved in with the family and helped Thomas Lincoln on the farm.

Abraham and Sarah worked hard with their father on the farm. Then in 1819, a year after Nancy Lincoln died, Thomas Lincoln traveled to Elizabethtown, Kentucky. Reasons for the trip are unclear, but perhaps Thomas was lonely. In Elizabethtown he contacted Sarah Bush Johnston, a woman he had known before he married Nancy. Johnston was a widow, and Lincoln asked her to marry him and return with him to Indiana. She agreed and the two were married in Elizabethtown on December 2, 1819.

From the day of her arrival, Sarah brightened the Lincoln family's life. She brought her three children to join the household, and Abraham and Sarah got along well with Elizabeth, John D., and Matilda Johnston. Unlike the cruel stepmothers of fairy tales, Sarah Lincoln was loving and kind. She kept all her children clean and well fed, and she encouraged the sometimes moody Abraham.

For a few months during warm weather, the Lincoln

children walked several miles to a one-room, windowless schoolhouse. The school was called a blab school, because the pupils learned their lessons by repeating them out loud.

At school, Abraham Lincoln learned reading, writing, and arithmetic. Abe continued his education on his own, reading every book he could find. He read and memorized most of the books his stepmother brought with her when she married his father. Abe's favorites included the Bible, *Aesop's Fables*, *Lessons in Elocution*, and a *History of the United States*, which began with the discovery of America and ended with the annexation of Florida.[3] He also read Shakespeare and the poetry of Robert Burns.

Abe also wrote poetry of his own. Some of his poems showed his dry sense of humor. For example, in his math sum book he wrote, "Abraham Lincoln is my name / And with my pen I wrote the same / I wrote in both hast [sic] and speed / and left it here for fools to read."[4]

His darker moods were also recorded in verse. When he was seventeen he wrote: "Time what an empty vaper [sic] / tis and days how swift they are swift as an indian arr[ow] / fly on like a shooting star the present moment Just [is here] / then slides away in h[as]te that we [can] never say they['re ours] / but [only say] th[ey]'re past."[5]

Abe did well in school, but he worked hard to learn. He once said of his mind that it was "very hard to scratch anything on it and almost impossible after you get it there to rub it out."[6]

As he grew older, Lincoln knew that he did not want to spend his life in backbreaking labor, as his father had. He continued to live and work at home, but he slowly withdrew from his father. He hired out for farmwork and worked at other odd jobs, such as splitting rails for fences, butchering hogs, skinning raccoons, and ferrying travelers across the Ohio River.

When Lincoln was seventeen, his sister, Sarah, married Aaron Grigsby, a neighbor. One year later she died in childbirth. His sister's death further weakened Lincoln's ties to home.

At eighteen, Lincoln was hired by a storekeeper to take a flatboat loaded with farm supplies twelve hundred miles down the Ohio and Mississippi rivers to New Orleans, Louisiana. This was the lanky farm boy's first trip to a big city, and he was amazed at everything he saw there.

In 1830, when he was twenty-one, Lincoln helped his father and stepmother move to Macon County, Illinois. Since he was now legally of age, he no longer owed his father his labor. When Denton Offutt, a businessman in New Salem, Illinois, offered Lincoln a job transporting goods to New Orleans in the spring of 1831, he accepted. With this trip, Lincoln left his father's house for good.

In the future, he kept in touch with his stepmother, but he had little contact with his father and seldom spoke of him. In 1851, when Lincoln was told that his father was dying, he did not travel from Springfield,

SOURCE DOCUMENT

A sample of Lincoln's poetry, written in 1844, after a visit to southern Indiana, where his mother and sister were buried.

Illinois, to his father's home in Coles County, Illinois, to see him. He asked his stepbrother, John D. Johnston, to tell his father "that if we could meet now, it is doubtful whether it would not be more painful than pleasant."[7]

Historians have speculated that perhaps Abraham Lincoln and his father were not close because father and son did little else together except work. Reportedly, Thomas Lincoln showed little affection for his son. Some sources say that he sometimes threw away young Abraham's books and beat him for reading instead of working, or for correcting or interrupting him during a conversation.[8]

When Lincoln left home for good at twenty-one, he had barely a year of formal education and no special skills. He did not know what he wanted to do, but he thought he might become a businessman. After the New Orleans trip, he returned to New Salem, where Offutt promised to stock a store and make Lincoln the manager. While he waited for Offutt to open his store, Lincoln worked at any job he could find. Men who could do hard labor were always in demand on the frontier.

New Salem, Illinois, located on the Sangamon River, was two years old and growing. Residents hoped their fast-growing town would become a center for river travel and trade.

In September 1831, Offutt finally opened his store and hired Lincoln as his assistant. The young man soon earned a name as an honest and capable storekeeper. Offutt boasted around town that his new helper,

Abraham Lincoln, was not only the smartest man around but also the strongest. Lincoln was tall and thin, but years of hard physical labor had made him strong. This led to a dare from Jack Armstrong, the leader of a group of rough young men from a neighboring town who called themselves the Clary's Grove boys. Armstrong was a fine wrestler, and he challenged Lincoln to a match. Lincoln accepted. It is uncertain who won the contest. One version of the tale said that Armstrong tricked Lincoln and won. Another said that Lincoln not only threw Armstrong but then had to wrestle all of the Clary's Grove boys. Whatever the outcome, Lincoln's acceptance of Armstrong's dare earned him the respect and praise of the New Salem townspeople, as well as that of the Clary's Grove boys.

While he was working in Offutt's store, Lincoln joined the New Salem debating club. He became a popular speaker because his talks were full of engaging and funny stories.

As they grew better acquainted with him, New Salem townspeople thought the kind, good-humored, hardworking Abraham Lincoln would be a good spokesperson for their town. They convinced him to run for the state legislature. This decision proved to be one of the most important of the young man's life.

This painting, called "Lincoln the Rail Splitter," was done by J.L.C. Ferris. It dramatizes the legend of Lincoln as a rural frontier laborer.

3

POLITICAL AMBITIONS

I n March 1832, Abraham Lincoln ran for the Illinois House of Representatives. Then, men who ran for local public office did not need experience or the backing of parties. Lincoln simply declared his candidacy in the New Salem newspaper, the *Sangamo Journal*.

Lincoln told the voters that, as a state legislator, he would work to improve the Sangamon River, so boats could more easily carry goods. The increase in river traffic would help New Salem's economy and bring in new settlers. He said he was against banks' high interest rates for loans and that he wanted to improve education.[1] He did not explain how he would make the improvements, how much his programs would cost, or how the money would be raised.

Lincoln ended on a personal note. He said he had "no wealthy or popular relations to recommend" him, but if elected, voters "will have conferred a favor upon" him that he vowed to repay. "But if the good people in their wisdom shall see fit to keep me in the background," he said, "I have been too familiar with disappointments to be very much chagrined."[2]

Shortly after Lincoln announced his candidacy, Offutt's many businesses failed, including the store where Lincoln worked.

In April 1832, Lincoln was looking for work when the Black Hawk War broke out. Chief Black Hawk had led the Sauk and Fox tribes back to northwestern Illinois from reservations west of the Mississippi. He claimed his people simply wanted to raise corn along the Rock River, but the move violated a treaty made the year before.[3] Illinois Governor John Reynolds called for all volunteers to fight the Native Americans and Lincoln enlisted in the state militia. Then, states had fighting units called militia that were separate from the United States Army and Navy.

State militia officers were elected by the men they would command. During his first one-month enlistment, Lincoln ran for captain of his company. He was elected by a wide margin. Lincoln served as a private during two subsequent one-month reenlistments.

During the three months Lincoln was in the militia, he did not see a hostile Native American or fire a single shot. He did not go home a war hero, but the important friends he made and the $125 in pay he earned made his time in the militia profitable.

Lincoln's horse was stolen soon after his discharge from the militia on July 10, 1832, so he walked most of the way home. He arrived back in New Salem too late in the year to conduct a winning political campaign. When the votes were counted, Lincoln came in eighth in a field of thirteen candidates.[4] The four candidates who received the most votes were elected to office. Lincoln was not among them.

After his political defeat, Lincoln again needed work. He thought about becoming a blacksmith, but the hard labor did not appeal to him. He also considered becoming a lawyer. He was interested in the law and often attended court sessions. He had read a few law books and knew how to prepare simple legal papers, but he did not think he had enough education to pursue a career in law.

While Lincoln was trying to decide what to do next, James and J. Rowan Herndon put their New Salem general store up for sale. Lincoln and William F. Berry, who had served in Lincoln's company during the Black Hawk War, bought the store together. Neither Berry nor Lincoln had the cash to pay for the store, but they signed notes promising to pay when they could. The two partners then signed more notes to purchase the stock from two more stores that were going out of business. Lincoln was, once again, a storekeeper. He was also deeply in debt.

The Lincoln-Berry store did not make money. Because of changing economic conditions, many settlers had moved away from New Salem to find work. As a result, the town was no longer growing. Several New Salem businesses closed. Lincoln and his partner, Berry, also went out of business. When Berry died three years later, in 1835, Lincoln assumed the partnership's debts.

Again, Lincoln took odd jobs. He farmed, split rails for fence posts with an ax, served on juries, clerked at elections, and carried poll sheets to Springfield. Then, friends recommended him for the postmaster's position. Lincoln was appointed by President Andrew Jackson to fill the vacant postmaster office. The job paid a small wage, and it allowed Lincoln to read newspapers before customers picked them up at the Lincoln-Berry store.

Lincoln also became deputy surveyor for the county. Both jobs helped his political career because he met people who might later vote for him. People in the county knew him as a dependable, likable man. He often helped settle land-boundary disputes, witnessed business or legal matters, and composed letters for others.

When Lincoln first ran for office, most voters were either Democrats or Whigs. Democratic candidates generally agreed with President Andrew Jackson's stand: get rid of the national bank, resist high tariffs on imported goods, and limit federal funds spent on internal improvements, such as roads and canals. Members of the Whig party were usually anti-Jackson and took the opposite side on these issues.

Before he became a candidate for office, the twenty-five-year-old Lincoln had not declared himself a member of either party, but he agreed more often with the Whigs than with the Democrats. In addition, he had favored Andrew Jackson's opponent, Henry Clay, in the 1832 presidential contest. In the 1834 election, Lincoln ran as a Whig candidate. He received support from members of both the Whig and Democratic parties, because voters at that time seldom voted along party lines. Instead, they chose candidates whose views they agreed with and whom they liked and respected.

As a result, Lincoln was one of the four candidates elected to the state legislature in 1834. In November, wearing the first suit he had ever owned, he set off for his first legislative session at the state capitol in Vandalia, Illinois.

At about this time Lincoln decided to study law, since he thought reading law would help him with his duties as a state legislator. John Todd Stuart—a lawyer, a Whig, and a state legislator whom Lincoln had met during the Black Hawk War—encouraged his friend. He loaned Lincoln the law books he needed to study.

The Illinois legislature met in Vandalia from December 1, 1834, to February 13, 1835. Most of the state's business concerned such everyday issues as name changes, killing wolves, naming county surveyors, or giving permission to couples to divorce. Lincoln faithfully attended meetings, but at first he was silent, choosing to follow the lead of Stuart and other more experienced lawmakers. As the session wore on, however, he entered into the debates. He was soon asked to write out the laws as they were made.

After Lincoln completed his first term in the state legislature early in 1835, he returned to New Salem a few hundred dollars richer. The notes he had signed when he and Berry bought their store were coming due, however, and his legislator's salary was not enough to cover his debts.

Lincoln's debt bothered him. "That debt was the greatest obstacle I have ever met in life," he once told a friend. "I had no way of speculating, and could not earn money except by labor, and to earn by labor eleven hundred dollars, besides my living, seemed the work of a lifetime. There was, however, but one way. I went to the creditors and told them that if they would let me alone, I would give them all I could earn over my living, as fast as I could earn it."[5] Lincoln kept his word, but it would be several years before he paid off his debts.

In 1836, Lincoln again ran as a Whig candidate for the Illinois House of Representatives. He was well known in Sangamon County, and in the August election he received more votes than any other candidate. He was one of nine Whigs elected to represent Sangamon County in the state legislature.

The nine elected Whigs—seven representatives and two senators—called themselves the Long Nine, because they were all at least six feet tall. They claimed that if laid end-to-end, they would stretch fifty-five feet.

The nine elected candidates were Abraham Lincoln, John Dawson, Daniel Stone, Ninian W. Edwards, William F. Elkins, R. L. Wilson, Andrew McCormick, Job Fletcher, and Arthur Herndon.[6]

The Long Nine, with Lincoln as their leader, wanted to move the state capital from Vandalia to the larger and more centrally located city of Springfield. Other legislators did not want the capital moved at all, or favored moving it to a city other than Springfield. Usher Ferguson Linder, a representative from Coles County, Illinois, was a leader in an attempt by other legislators to reduce the influence of the Long Nine. A proposal by Linder to restructure some Illinois counties was intended to cut the number of elected representatives from Sangamon County.

This proposal was killed in the Senate, but Linder then proposed to investigate the Illinois State Bank, located in Springfield. Such an investigation might have closed the bank, lessening Springfield's chances of becoming the state capital. Lincoln and the other Sangamon County legislators were, of course, opposed. This measure was also defeated. A bill was finally passed to move the capital. Springfield was chosen as the new capital city of Illinois in February 1837.

When the legislative session ended that March, Lincoln returned to New Salem for the last time. He had earned his license to practice law in September, and in April 1837 he moved to Springfield. He and John Todd Stuart had agreed to practice law as partners.

Within months after Lincoln moved to Springfield, the few remaining residents of New Salem also moved on, leaving behind a ghost town.

Lincoln had finally found a career that would provide a home, a steady income, and freedom from debt. As an attorney, he would no longer wander from place to place, hiring out for whatever backbreaking labor he could find.

4

THE LAW AND POLITICS

Between sessions of the Illinois state legislature, Lincoln studied law. At that time, attorneys did not need college degrees, but simply read law books to become licensed. To become licensed, Lincoln also needed a certificate of good character, which he received from Judge Stephen T. Logan on March 24, 1836.[1] In September 1836, two justices of the Illinois Supreme Court licensed him to practice law. On March 1, 1837, the clerk of the Illinois Supreme Court entered Lincoln's name on the state's list of attorneys.[2]

Twenty-eight-year-old Abraham Lincoln rode into Springfield on a borrowed horse in April 1837, carrying all of his belongings in two saddlebags. He had seven dollars in his pocket and owed more than one thousand dollars.[3] He stopped at a general store to ask the price of a mattress and bedding. He admitted to the storekeeper, twenty-two-year-old Joshua Speed, that he did not have the seventeen dollars the goods would cost. Speed had heard one of Lincoln's political speeches and respected him.[4] He saw that the newcomer hated to ask for credit, so he told Lincoln that he could stay with him, in a room over the store, until he could afford a place of his own. Lincoln gratefully accepted Speed's offer. Thus began a lasting friendship between the two men.

Springfield had many law offices, so most attorneys looked beyond the city for clients. Twice a year, a judge traveled about five hundred miles to hear cases in the fourteen Illinois county seats. The area covered was called the Eighth Circuit. Like most Springfield attorneys, Lincoln and John Todd Stuart followed the circuit court judge, representing clients in towns along the way.

For six months each year Lincoln traveled the Eighth Circuit. He and the other lawyers who rode the circuit on horseback visited with settlers and slept on farmhouse floors or shared a bed in simple hotels called roadhouses. The traveling lawyers advised each other on how to plead a case. At the end of a day in court, they sat around the fire in a general store or tavern and told stories, sang songs, or played cards.

Lincoln was well liked by the people he met. They said he was strong, tall, and awkward but told funny stories and jokes. They also said he was pleasant and kind, but he could be silent and sad. He was always looking for a chance to learn and to help friends or strangers in trouble.[5] He was sometimes called Honest Abe.

Lincoln's constant contact with the voters in Sangamon County and the Eighth Circuit helped his political career. Every two years he took time out from his law practice to run for the state legislature. He was easily reelected to the Illinois House of Representatives in August 1838.

As a state lawmaker, Lincoln introduced bills to incorporate Springfield and to get state funds for building a new statehouse. He also continued to push for new and improved state highways, railroads, and canals. He and other members of the Long Nine supported the Internal Improvements Act, a plan calling for projects that would cost an estimated $12 million. Construction was begun, but plans fell through when the economic panic of 1837 hit and state funds dried up.

Lincoln had become a party man. He saw that the backing of a strong political party could elect a candidate to office. Once elected, that candidate might bring about desirable changes. Lincoln led the Whigs in the Illinois state legislature and worked hard for the party in every election. He campaigned for Stuart, his law partner and fellow Whig, when Stuart ran for the United States House of Representatives against Democrat Stephen A. Douglas. Stuart won by thirty-six votes.

When the Whigs nominated William Henry Harrison to run against Democrat Martin Van Buren for president in 1840, Lincoln organized Whigs in Illinois to back Harrison. National voter turnout reached 80 percent for the November election, and Harrison was elected.

During the years that Lincoln studied law, served as a state legislator, and helped strengthen the Whig party, the slavery issue was heating up. In the South, a person could be hanged for speaking out against slavery or for inciting slaves to riot. In the North, the Underground Railroad helped runaway slaves escape to Canada.[6] The Underground Railroad was a system in which people called conductors provided food, shelter, and transportation to fugitive slaves.

Everywhere violence erupted over slavery. Around 1833, antiabolitionist rioters in Philadelphia damaged four houses and a church and killed two African-American men. A Quaker, Benjamin Lundy, who spoke out against slavery, was beaten by a mob in Baltimore. In Boston at a meeting of the Female Antislavery Society, a troublemaker had to be rescued by the police when others in the crowd attacked. In 1836, Elijah Lovejoy, an outspoken minister who was against slavery, tried to start a newspaper in Alton, Illinois. A group of local people led by Usher F. Linder, now the state attorney general, strongly opposed Lovejoy's newspaper.[7] Twice, mobs threw his printing press into the river. On November 7, 1837, Lovejoy was shot and killed by a mob.[8]

During Lincoln's second term in the state legislature, he and other legislators were asked by several states to pass a resolution against abolitionists, stating that the United States Constitution supported slavery. They were also asked to declare that slavery was entirely a state matter and that the District of Columbia could not legally abolish slavery. Lincoln and five other legislators voted against the resolution. Seventy-seven others voted for it and it passed.

Lincoln and Dan Stone, a fellow Whig legislator, wrote a protest after the resolution was passed. They said "that the institution of slavery is founded on both injustice and bad policy, but that the promulgation [teaching] of abolition doctrines tends rather to increase than abate its evils." They added that they believed that Congress had "no power under the Constitution to interfere with the institution of slavery in the different States." Congress, however, did have the power to abolish slavery in the District of Columbia, although it "ought not to be exercised unless at the request of the people" of D.C.[9]

Acts of violence over slavery may have inspired a speech Lincoln gave at Springfield on January 27, 1838, at a meeting of the Young Men's Lyceum, a debating society. In his talk, titled, "The Perpetuation of Our Political Institutions," he called upon Americans to restore law and order, lest the nation be torn apart from within. "Passion has helped us," he said, "but can do so no more. It will in [the] future be our enemy. Reason, cold, calculating, unimpassioned reason, must furnish all the materials for our future support and defence [sic]."[10]

After eight years in the Illinois legislature, Lincoln wanted to move on to higher office. He wanted to serve in the United States Congress in Washington, D.C.

5

FAMILY AND POLITICS

By 1839, Abraham Lincoln was a well-known attorney and politician. He was also one of Springfield's most eligible bachelors. Although he was awkward and shy around women, Lincoln was often invited to parties where he was introduced to single ladies seeking suitable husbands.

Ninian Edwards, one of the Long Nine, and his wife, Elizabeth Todd Edwards, often gave parties at their home in Springfield. Lincoln was usually among the bachelors who were invited.

When Elizabeth Edwards's younger sister, Mary Todd, came for a visit in 1839, she soon became popular. Mary, at twenty-one, was a small, friendly woman with dark brown hair and blue eyes. One of four daughters of Robert Todd, a wealthy Kentucky banker, Mary had been raised in luxury. She had attended a private school in Lexington and was well educated.

Soon after her arrival at her sister's home, Mary was courted by several Springfield bachelors. One of those whom Mary dated was Stephen A. Douglas, the leading Democrat in Illinois and a political foe of Lincoln's. Abraham Lincoln was also among Mary's eager suitors.

Although Lincoln had fewer social graces than some of the other men who courted Mary, he was honest and kind, and he and Mary Todd had several interests in common. Both were from Kentucky, and both were Whigs. They both enjoyed the poetry of Robert Burns, and both had a lively sense of humor.

Before Mary Todd, Lincoln probably had little experience in matters of the heart. In 1837, however, he almost married Mary Owens, a Kentucky woman who had been introduced to him by her sister. He and Miss Owens became engaged, but Lincoln had second thoughts. In a polite letter to Miss Owens, he said he doubted she would be happy with him. She would be poor if she married him and she deserved better. Lincoln said he would keep his promise to marry her if she wanted. "I want, at this particular time, more than anything else, to do right with you," he wrote, "and if I *knew* it would be doing right, as I rather suspect it would, to let you alone, I would do it."[1] He would understand if she changed her mind. "If it suits you best to not answer this—farewell," he continued, "a long life and a merry one attend you."[2] Mary Owens did not answer the letter, thus ending the romance.

Perhaps by the time Lincoln met Mary Todd, he was more self-confident. The couple became engaged in December 1840. Then, once again, Lincoln had second thoughts about marriage. In January 1841, he broke his engagement to Mary Todd.[3]

After he broke his engagement, Lincoln plunged into a deep depression. He had suffered from depression most of his life. At that time, such dark moods were called melancholia, hypochondria, or "the hypo." Today his condition would probably be called clinical depression. Biographers have said that Lincoln's bouts with depression might have been caused by the loss, early in his life, of his younger brother, his mother, and his sister.[4]

The depression that began with Lincoln's broken engagement lasted several weeks. It further saddened him that his closest friend, Joshua Speed, had recently sold his store and returned to Kentucky. Legislative sessions began before Lincoln could recover from his depression, but he attended daily. "I am now the most miserable man living," he wrote to John Todd Stuart.[5]

Despite his condition, Lincoln continued working. In April 1841, Stephen Trigg Logan asked Lincoln to become his junior law partner. The new partnership improved Lincoln's income as well as his outlook. His depression finally lifted when, in August 1841, he visited Speed and his mother and sister at their home in Louisville, Kentucky.

A few months after Lincoln's visit, Speed married a young woman named Fanny Henning. He wrote to Lincoln about the joys of married life, and Lincoln was encouraged by his friend's happiness. Shortly thereafter, he and Mary Todd met at a friend's party and began dating again. Lincoln again proposed and Mary accepted. Mary and Abraham were married in the Edwards's parlor on November 4, 1842, by the Reverend Charles Dresser. Lincoln was thirty-three and Mary Todd was twenty-three.

The newlyweds moved into a rented room over Springfield's Globe Tavern, the best hotel in town. There they paid four dollars a week. This price included both

Mary Todd Lincoln (left) and Abraham Lincoln (right) around 1846, four years after their marriage. Both photos were probably taken by N.H. Shepherd, a Springfield photographer. This is the earliest known photo of Mrs. Lincoln.

room and board.[6] On August 1, 1843, the Lincolns' first son, Robert, was born.

In the spring of 1844, Abraham and Mary Lincoln purchased a house in Springfield from Reverend Dresser. They paid twelve hundred dollars for the house and gave Dresser a small lot that Lincoln owned, worth about three hundred dollars.[7] The house on the corner of Eighth and Jackson streets was the only home Mr. and Mrs. Lincoln owned during their married life.

Both the Lincolns worked hard—Abraham as an attorney and Mary in their home—but money was scarce. For at least three months out of the year, Lincoln traveled the Eighth Judicial Circuit. He still paid regularly on the debt that he owed. While her husband was away, Mary took care of Robert and all the household chores. Her duties increased when, on March 10, 1846, another son, Edward Baker Lincoln, was born.

In 1844, Stephen Logan wanted to become partners with his son, so Lincoln left the partnership. The parting was friendly, and for years Logan and Lincoln occasionally worked together.

Shortly after the Logan-Lincoln partnership ended, Lincoln asked William Herndon, a young man nine years his junior who had studied law with him, to become his partner. "Billy, I can trust you, if you can trust me,"[8] Lincoln said. That partnership lasted nearly seventeen years, until Lincoln's death.

The law firm of Lincoln and Herndon did well. As the junior partner in the firm, Herndon had his own clients and argued cases in court. Lincoln handled routine paperwork and research, talked to clients, and also argued cases. He won many of his cases, so his services were in demand. From the beginning of his career until 1854, he represented more than 330 cases before the Illinois Supreme Court.[9]

Lincoln's term in the 1841 Illinois General Assembly was his last, because he wanted to run for a seat in the the United States House of Representatives. He struck an apparent arrangement with two other Whigs in his Illinois district, to take turns running for Congress. Edward D. Baker was elected to the House in 1842. He agreed that after serving his term, he would step down. After completing his two-year term in 1844, Baker stepped down to allow John J. Hardin to run. Abraham Lincoln's turn would come in 1846. In 1846, however, Hardin did not want to step down, and Lincoln fought to win his party's nomination.

Lincoln won the 1846 election on August 3, running against Democrat Peter Cartwright, a Methodist minister. Congress did not meet until December 1847, so it was over a year before Lincoln took office. He, Mary, and the two boys arrived in Washington, D.C., on December 2, 1847.

The Lincolns rented rooms in a boardinghouse in Washington, and Abraham began his term in the United States House of Representatives. He was a well-known Whig in his home state, but he was the only member of his party elected from Illinois. Therefore, he had little influence with President James K. Polk, a Democrat. Lincoln did not agree with Polk's Jacksonian policies. He favored instead the views of Whig leader Henry Clay, who had been defeated by Andrew Jackson in the 1832 presidential election.

As Lincoln began his term in the House, the Whig party was splitting up, partly because the strong party leaders were aging: Senator Henry Clay was seventy years old in 1847; Senator Daniel Webster was sixty-five. Eighty-year-old congressman and former President John Quincy Adams died early in the House session.

During his two-year term in Congress, Lincoln worked to revive the flagging Whig party. He spoke for such standard party issues as protective tariffs and internal improvements—roads, canals, and railroads. The National Bank was a dead issue, since the charter for the Second Bank of the United States had not been renewed under President Jackson.

Congressman Lincoln also helped elect Whig presidential candidate General Zachary Taylor. For political reasons, Lincoln was against President Polk's war with Mexico, which was fought over the addition of Texas to the United States. He spoke against the war to Congress, hoping to weaken the Democrats' chances in the next presidential election.

Throughout Lincoln's term in Congress, slavery was an important concern. Many congressmen, including Lincoln, thought that the practice would die out in the United States if new territories and states did not allow it. Lincoln believed that slavery was the one issue that could split the Union.[10]

Between sessions of Congress, the Lincoln family went home to Springfield. In the 1848 presidential election Lincoln campaigned hard for Whig candidate General Zachary Taylor, against the Democratic candidate, Lewis Cass. Taylor defeated Cass.

During his two-year term in Congress, Lincoln was successful in his goal to help elect Taylor to the presidency. He also earned a name among his fellow congressmen as an excellent speaker. He failed, however, to revive the Whig party. It had not united behind new issues and had split into many weak factions.

Lincoln kept his word not to run for reelection to the House. Back home in Springfield, some of Lincoln's friends urged him to seek an appointment as commissioner of the General Land Office. The position was powerful, because the commissioner was in charge of all public lands. In addition, the job paid three thousand dollars a year—a large sum at that time and more than Lincoln was likely to earn as a lawyer.[11] Lincoln showed little interest in the position until he heard that Justin Butterfield, a Whig lawyer from Chicago, could be appointed. Since Butterfield had not supported Taylor in his bid for the presidency, Lincoln saw his appointment as a "political blunder."[12]

Lincoln entered the race. He asked supporters to write letters on his behalf, and he traveled to Washington, D.C., to plead his case. President Taylor delayed the appointment for three weeks to consider both men, but the position went to Butterfield.

Lincoln then turned down an offer to serve as governor of the Oregon Territory, citing Mary's reluctance to move. He resumed his law practice with William Herndon. It seemed his career in public office was over.

6

VICTORY AND CONFLICT

Tragedy struck soon after Lincoln returned to Illinois from Washington, D.C. On February 1, 1850, shortly before his fourth birthday, Edward Lincoln died after a long illness. The 1850 United States Census listed the cause of the child's death as "consumption." Today it would probably be listed as tuberculosis, a bacterial infection of the lungs.

Lincoln mourned his son's death deeply but silently. Mary Lincoln, already worn down from caring for Eddie during his final illness, was ill with grief.

The Lincolns' third son, William Wallace, was born on December 21, 1850. "Willie" was a good-natured, intelligent boy and his parents adored him. Thomas Lincoln, their fourth and last son, was born on April 4, 1853. Like most babies, Thomas had a head which was

45

too large for his tiny body, prompting his father to call him Tadpole. As the baby grew, his body caught up with his head, but for the rest of his life, Thomas Lincoln was called Tad.

After his term in Congress ended, Lincoln seemed to have lost interest in politics. Although he campaigned for Whig political candidates, he did not run for office himself. Then, in 1854, Congress passed the Kansas-Nebraska Act, which repealed the 1820 Missouri Compromise. After passage of the act, Lincoln declared himself "thunderstruck" and "stunned."[1] He was roused to political action.

The Missouri Compromise, passed in 1820, admitted

An 1860 photograph of Lincoln's first and only house at Eighth and Jackson streets in Springfield, Illinois. Lincoln and his son Tad are standing inside the fence at the corner of the house.

Missouri to the Union as a slave state. An amendment attached to the bill banned slavery in all remaining Louisiana Purchase territories north of the fortieth parallel. The bill was so named because it was a compromise between Southern states that wanted slavery in new territories and Northern states that were against the spread of slavery. For thirty-four years the Missouri Compromise had kept the peace over the issue of slavery in new territories.

The Kansas-Nebraska Act of 1854 contradicted the Missouri Compromise. Sponsored by Senator Stephen A. Douglas, head of the Senate Committee on Territories, the act was supposed to settle the question of allowing slavery in what is now Kansas and Nebraska. Douglas called for "popular sovereignty." This meant residents of the Kansas and Nebraska territories could vote on whether or not to allow slavery. Slave states were for the act, because they wanted slavery in the new territories. Free states were against it, because they did not want slavery to be permitted in any new territory. The act reopened the national slavery debate. It also split the Democratic and Whig parties.

When Southern Whigs supported the Kansas-Nebraska Act, most Northern Whigs left the party to join the newly formed Republican party. (Those Southern Whigs who left the party joined the Democratic party.) Some former Whigs who opposed slavery joined the Know-Nothing party. The Know-Nothings were against the Roman Catholic Church and all forms of immigration, including importing slaves. Members were called "Know-Nothings" because they met in secret, and when asked about their party they always answered, "I don't know."[2] By the end of 1855, the Whig party was no longer a strong political organization.[3]

Lincoln was against the Kansas-Nebraska Act because he felt that slavery should be kept out of all new territories and states. "It is wrong," he said, "wrong in its direct effect, letting slavery into Kansas and Nebraska—and wrong in its prospective principle, allowing it to spread to every other part of the wide world, where men can be found inclined to take it."[4]

Lincoln's opposition to the Kansas-Nebraska Act moved him to run for nomination to the Illinois state legislature. Once nominated, senators were chosen by the state legislature. In 1854, he succeeded in winning a seat. Lincoln soon changed his mind and resigned, however, because he decided he wanted to run for the United States Senate.

Lincoln ran for the dying Whig party's nomination to the United States Senate in February 1855, but was defeated by the Democratic candidate, Lyman Trumbull. After this defeat, he helped organize the Republican party in Illinois. He officially joined the party in 1856.

The Republican party held its first national convention in Philadelphia in June 1856. At the convention, Republicans nominated John C. Frémont, who explored the Rocky Mountains and the West, to run for president of the United States against the

SOURCE DOCUMENT

434. A portuguese captain, on the coast of
Guinea, seizes a few African beings
and sells them in the South of Spain—

501-2-3. Slaves are carried from Africa to
the Spanish Colonies in America—

516-17. Charles 5.th of Spain gives encourage-
ments to the African Slave trade—

562. John Hawkins carries slaves to the
British West Indies—

620. A dutch ship carries a cargo of African
slaves to Virginia—

624. Slaves introduced into New-York—

630 to 41. Slaves introduced into Massachusetts.

776. The period of our revolution, there
were about 600,000 slaves in
the Colonies; and there are now in
the U.S. about 3¼ millions—

Soto, the catholic confessor of Charles 5. opposed
Slavery and the Slave trade from the beginning,
and, in 1543, procures from the King some ameli-
oration of its rigors—

The American colonies, from the beginning, appealed
to the British crown against the Slave trade, but
without success—

1727. Quakers begin to agitate for the abolition
of Slavery within their own denomination—

Notes on slavery, written by Lincoln in January 1855. He wrote the notes before one of his many speeches, as he tried to organize his thoughts and opinions on the subject.

Democratic candidate, James Buchanan. Lincoln gave more than fifty speeches for the Republicans.[5] James Buchanan won the election.

About this time, a case involving a slave named Dred Scott was decided by the United States Supreme Court. On March 6, 1857, two days after President Buchanan's inauguration, the Supreme Court issued a decision in the case, which had been pending for several years.

Dred Scott was a slave owned by John Emerson of Missouri. In 1836, Emerson took Scott to Minnesota, a territory where slavery had been banned by the terms of the Missouri Compromise. Then Emerson moved back to Missouri without Scott. After Emerson died, Scott sued Emerson's widow for his freedom. He claimed that since he lived in a free territory, he should be released from slavery. The 1857 Supreme Court held that the government had no power to make citizens slave or free. It also said that since the Constitution did not make slaves citizens, they had no right to sue in federal court. When Supreme Court Justice Roger Brooke Taney wrote the majority opinion for the court, he added that the Missouri Compromise violated the Constitution.

Lincoln criticized the court's ruling. He said the court had ignored the Declaration of Independence, which "was held sacred by all, and thought to include all."[6] The Dred Scott decision widened the gap between North and South and has been listed as one of the major causes of the Civil War.[7]

In 1858, Senator Stephen A. Douglas, a Democrat

and long one of Lincoln's political foes, was up for reelection to a third term in the United States Senate. At that time, Americans did not vote directly for United States senators. They were chosen by members of the state legislature. Not until 1913 did voters gain the right to elect United States senators directly. Lincoln hoped to win Douglas's Senate seat by persuading people to vote for the Republican candidates for the Illinois legislature. Republican legislators would, in turn, elect him to Congress. Douglas had to convince voters to choose Democratic candidates for the legislature, who would then reelect him to the Senate.

At the Republican convention held June 16, 1858, in Springfield, Illinois, Abraham Lincoln was chosen as his party's candidate for the United States Senate, to run against Douglas. At the end of the convention Lincoln delivered his "House Divided" speech that included these famous lines:

> A house divided against itself cannot stand.
>
> I believe this government cannot endure, permanently half *slave* and half *free*.
>
> I do not expect the Union to be *dissolved*—I do not expect the house to *fall*—but I *do* expect it will cease to be divided.
>
> It will become all one thing, or all the other.
>
> Either the *opponents* of slavery, will arrest the further spread of it, and place it where the public mind shall rest in the belief that it is in course of ultimate extinction; or its *advocates* will push it forward, till it

shall become alike lawful in all the States, *old* as well as *new*—*North* as well as *South*.

Have we no tendency to the latter condition?[8]

Candidates Lincoln and Douglas were on opposite sides of the slavery question. Unlike Lincoln, Douglas agreed with the Dred Scott decision. He also believed the people in Kansas and Nebraska should be allowed to vote on whether or not slavery would be permitted in those states—this is the concept of popular sovereignty.

During the campaign, whenever Douglas gave a speech, Lincoln spoke against Douglas's views. Finally, Lincoln proposed and Douglas agreed to a series of public debates on slavery. The two men would debate each other seven times, in seven different Illinois cities. They would argue the question: Is slavery morally wrong, or simply a matter to be voted in or out by citizens of the territories?

In the late summer and fall of 1858, huge crowds came to hear Honest Abe debate the Little Giant. (Douglas had been nicknamed the Little Giant because he was a giant in politics, but short in stature.)

In his speeches, Lincoln said that if America was to survive, the country could not accept slavery. "This is a world of compensations," he said, "and he who would *be* no slave, must consent to *have* no slave. Those who deny freedom to others, deserve it not for themselves."[9]

Lincoln and Douglas were equally skilled at debating. Douglas won the debates, however, if judged solely by the 1858 Illinois election results. The Democrats won

Stephen Douglas. This photograph of "the Little Giant" was taken at the time of the Lincoln-Douglas debates in 1858.

forty-six seats in the state legislature; forty-one went to Republicans. Eight more legislative seats that were not up for reelection in 1858 were also held by Democrats. This meant that in the vote for United States senator, Democratic votes outnumbered Republican votes and Douglas was reelected.[10]

During the 1858 debates, Lincoln assured Southerners that, should a Republican gain the White House in 1860, their way of life would not be threatened. On the other hand, he warned, if Southerners left the Union they would no longer be protected by the Constitution and they would lose any war that resulted.[11]

Despite Lincoln's words, some Southerners believed the Republicans wanted to destroy the South by putting an end to slavery. In October 1859, an event took place that many saw as proof. John Brown, a radical abolitionist, led eighteen men to Harpers Ferry, in what is now West Virginia, to free the slaves by force. The group took over the United States arsenal, but they did not attack the town.

Brown and his men were soon surrounded by United States Marines commanded by Colonel Robert E. Lee. In the battle that followed, Brown was wounded and ten of his men were killed. He surrendered and was arrested and charged with treason and murder. Brown was convicted and hanged on December 2, in Charlestown, West Virginia.[12] Despite Lincoln's insistence that "John Brown was no Republican,"[13] many Southerners believed otherwise. Although a

Lincoln as he appeared during the Lincoln-Douglas debates of 1858. Shortly after this photograph was taken, Lincoln grew a beard.

congressional investigation found no Republican involvement in Brown's actions, the incident added to the tension between North and South.[14]

At first, after Douglas defeated Lincoln for the United States Senate in 1858, Lincoln was depressed. He still had loyal supporters, however, and he felt better as he looked toward the future. "The cause of civil liberty must not be surrendered at the end of *one,* or even one *hundred* defeats," he remarked.[15]

Lincoln was a loyal Republican and had gained the attention of powerful party members. As a result, he won his party's nomination for president at the Republican National Convention in 1860.

Many working-class voters were drawn to Honest Abe, the "Rail Splitter." They saw him as a hardworking, self-made man who had risen from poverty. Many voters also liked Abraham Lincoln's stand against slavery and for economic development. In addition, some voters were tired of the do-nothing Democratic administration of President James Buchanan and thought Lincoln would be a welcome change. A split in the Democratic party had also hurt that party's chances of reclaiming the White House.

On November 6, 1860, fifty-one-year-old Abraham Lincoln won the election to become the sixteenth president of the United States. Hannibal Hamlin was elected vice-president. Lincoln defeated three opponents: John Breckinridge of the Southern Democrats, Stephen Douglas of the Northern Democrats, and John Bell of

SOURCE DOCUMENT

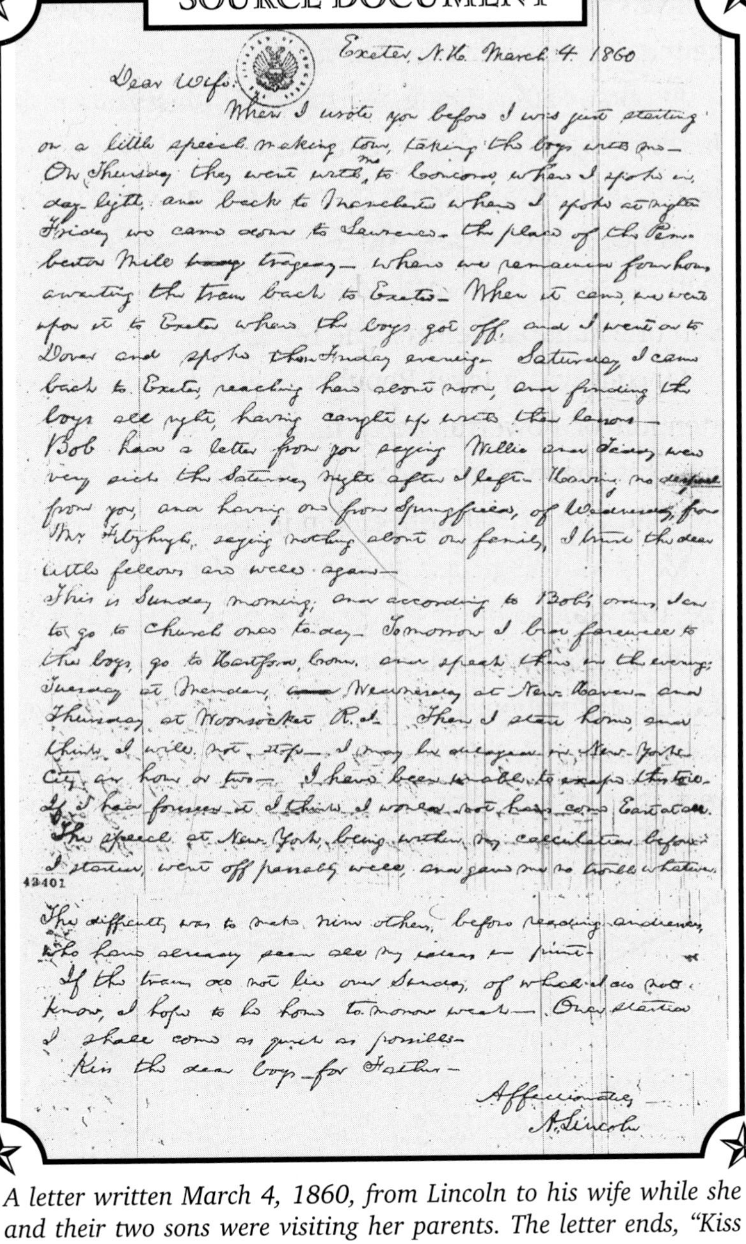

Exeter, N.H. March 4. 1860

Dear Wife:

When I wrote you before I was just starting on a little speech-making tour, taking the boys with me — On Thursday they went with me to Concord, where I spoke in day-light, and back to Manchester where I spoke at night. Friday we came down to Lawrence — the place of the Pemberton Mill ~~boy~~ tragedy — where we remained four hours awaiting the train back to Exeter — When it came, we went upon it to Exeter where the boys got off, and I went on to Dover and spoke there Friday evening. Saturday I came back to Exeter, reaching here about noon, and finding the boys all right, having caught up with their lessons —

Bob had a letter from you saying Willie and Taddy were very sick the Saturday night after I left — Having no despatch from you, and having one from Springfield, of Wednesday, from Mr. Fitzhugh, saying nothing about our family, I trust the dear little fellows are well again —

This is Sunday morning; and according to Bob's orders, I am to go to church once to-day — Tomorrow I bid farewell to the boys, go to Hartford, Conn. and speak there in the evening; Tuesday at Meriden, ~~and~~ Wednesday at New Haven — and Thursday at Woonsocket R.I. — Then I start home, and think I will not stop — I may be delayed in New-York City an hour or two — I have been unable to escape this toil. If I had foreseen it I think I would not have come East at all. The speech at New York, being within my calculation before I started, went off passably well and gave me no trouble whatever.

43401

The difficulty was to make nine others, before reading audiences, who had already seen all my ideas in print —

If the train does not lie over Sunday, of which I do not know, I hope to be home to-morrow week — Once started I shall come as quick as possible —

Kiss the dear boys for Father —

Affectionately

A. Lincoln

A letter written March 4, 1860, from Lincoln to his wife while she and their two sons were visiting her parents. The letter ends, "Kiss the dear boys for Father."

the Constitutional Union party. Lincoln received 180 electoral votes. Breckinridge received 72, Bell 39, and Douglas 12. Lincoln's name had not appeared on the ballot in states south of Virginia and Kentucky. He received just 39 percent of the popular vote.[16]

Southerners who could not accept Lincoln's antislavery, pro-Union course vowed to leave the Union.

7

A HOUSE DIVIDED

By the time President Lincoln took office on March 4, 1861, seven Southern states had voted to secede: Alabama, Florida, Georgia, Louisiana, Mississippi, South Carolina, and Texas. Arkansas, North Carolina, Tennessee, and Virginia left the Union within the following two months. Kentucky, Maryland, Missouri, and western Virginia were divided over the issue. Lincoln worked hard to keep them in the Union, however, and they did not secede. The western counties of Virginia opposed secession, while the rest of the state favored it. The western counties were admitted to the Union as the state of West Virginia in June 1863.[1]

President Lincoln delivered his first inaugural address on March 4, 1861, to a divided nation. He hoped his words would calm Southerners who were afraid of the future under a Republican president. At the same time, Lincoln said that "the Union of these States is perpetual."[2] Secession was illegal, he warned, and he was prepared to enforce the laws of the United States.

At the end of his speech, Lincoln tried to bring the South back into the Union. "We are not enemies, but friends," he said. "We must not be enemies. Though passion may have strained, it must not break our bonds of affection. The mystic chords of memory, stretching from every battlefield and patriot grave to every living heart and hearthstone, all over this broad land, will yet swell the chorus of the Union, when again touched, as surely they will be, by the better angels of our nature."[3] Lincoln's speech did not convince the South. In fact, for many Southerners the president's words meant that civil war was certain.

As the Southern states left the Union, rebel soldiers captured federal forts and arsenals, storehouses for arms and military equipment, within their borders. President James Buchanan, whom Lincoln replaced, did not take action against these seizures. When Lincoln took office, only Fort Sumter at Charleston, South Carolina, and Fort Pickens at Pensacola, Florida, were still under federal control in the South.

On the evening of the inaugural ball, President Lincoln was handed a note saying that Fort Sumter was surrounded by Confederate troops. The next morning, Lincoln learned that supplies at Fort Sumter would run out in six weeks. He had to decide whether to surrender the fort to the Confederate army or send new supplies.

Lincoln carefully weighed his choices. Should he surrender the fort to calm the Confederates? Or should he follow the suggestion of Assistant Secretary of the Navy Gustavus Fox and send Union ships with supplies? Lincoln met with his Cabinet. He finally decided to send the Union fleet with supplies, under Fox's command.

Lincoln sent a message to South Carolina Governor Francis Pickens that supplies for the fort were underway. On April 12, 1861, Confederate troops attacked Fort Sumter. The Civil War had officially begun. On April 14, Major Robert Anderson, commander of the fort, surrendered.

After the fall of Fort Sumter, President Lincoln asked for seventy-five thousand volunteers to fight against the Confederacy. He offered command of the Union troops to Robert E. Lee, but when Virginia, Lee's native state, seceded, Lee declined. Instead, he would lead the Confederate troops.

Union volunteers were slow to arrive in Washington, and people feared the city was in danger of attack. Troops coming to the capital had to pass through Maryland, a state where secession was still likely. On April 19, the 6th Massachusetts Infantry was attacked by an anti-Union mob in Baltimore. Thirteen were killed—nine civilians who were part of the attacking mob and four soldiers. They were the first to die in the Civil War. On April 25, the 7th New York Regiment arrived in Washington. When Massachusetts and Rhode Island troops followed days later, the city was protected.

In May 1861, Lincoln used his emergency war powers as president. Before Congress met in June, he called out the Army, ordered the Navy to place a blockade on Southern ports, enlarged the Army and Navy, and ordered the Department of Treasury to pay for his actions. He also suspended the writ of habeas corpus in certain areas. This action permitted military arrest, without showing cause, of persons suspected of treason. The right of habeas corpus is guaranteed by Article I, Section 9 of the United States Constitution. The term is Latin for "[that] you have the body." It is a court order that says that a jailer must bring a prisoner to court to determine whether or not imprisonment would be legal.

On May 28, Roger B. Taney, acting as a circuit judge, ruled that Lincoln's suspension of habeas corpus was unjustified. Lincoln ignored Taney's decision. As the Civil War progressed, he continued to use all the powers at his command as Commander in Chief.

In 1861, neither the North nor the South was ready to fight a war. With a population of about 18 million, the North had more men from which to recruit troops. (The North also had most of the country's manufacturing plants, but Southern crops provided raw materials.) Of the 9 million people in the South, 4 million were slaves. They could be forced to fight, but their loyalty to the Confederacy was questionable.[4] Fresh troops on both sides had to be enlisted, trained, and supplied, which took time.

At the beginning of the war, both sides relied on volunteers to fight. As the war continued, however, both the Union and the Confederacy had to resort to a military draft, or law that requires men of a certain age to join the military.

Commanders of the Union forces planned, at first, to capture Richmond, Virginia, the capital of the Confederacy. If they could take the capital, perhaps the South would be so discouraged that the war would end quickly.

In May 1861, Union soldiers captured Alexandria, Virginia. They then marched toward Manassas Junction, Virginia, a railroad center about thirty miles from Washington, D.C. Twenty-two thousand Confederate soldiers, under the command of General Pierre G. T. Beauregard, defended the city.

General Irvin McDowell led thirty thousand Union soldiers to fight the Confederates at Manassas. On July 21, in the First Battle of Bull Run, named for a creek near the battle site, the Confederates defeated the Union troops. The dead totaled 847. More than twenty-five hundred were wounded.[5]

At that point Lincoln most likely knew that the war would not be easily won. After the Union defeat, Lincoln demoted McDowell. He then named thirty-four-year-old General George Brinton McClellan commander of the Division of the Potomac, which included all of the Union troops in and around Washington, D.C.

General McClellan was liked by his men, but he was an arrogant man who resented President Lincoln's suggestions about military tactics. In fact, he sometimes referred to Lincoln as a "rare bird" and "the original Gorilla."[6] By fall, McClellan commanded a trained army of seventy thousand men. He was to capture Richmond by sea, then move on through Virginia. In October, Lincoln urged him to start his campaign. On November 1, he made McClellan general in chief, perhaps hoping the general would move if he had more authority.

By December 1861, McClellan still had not moved. He had heard exaggerated reports of the number of Confederate troops and likely did not want to risk defeat. In fact, McClellan had one hundred fifteen thousand soldiers, while the Confederate army numbered eighty-eight thousand.[7] McClellan fell ill with typhoid fever in December, and his army waited while he recovered.

On January 27, 1862, President Lincoln issued "General War Order No. 1," ordering General McClellan to move against the enemy on or before George Washington's birthday, February 22. Lincoln wanted Union forces to attack the railroad southwest of Manassas Junction, Virginia.

McClellan, however, wanted to attack Richmond, Virginia, by way of Chesapeake Bay. He talked Lincoln into waiting until this plan was ready. On March 11, 1862, McClellan's troops were finally on the move.

McClellan moved his army into the peninsula

General George B. McClellan, circa 1861. The "Napoleonic" pose (hand tucked inside the jacket) was popular at that time for photographs of members of the military.

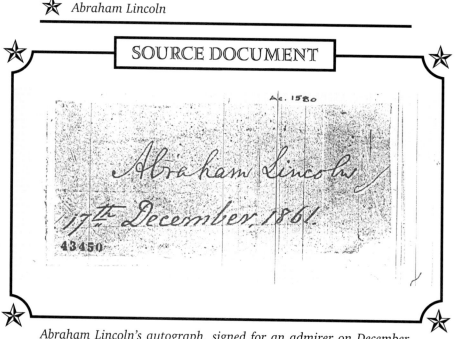

Abraham Lincoln's autograph, signed for an admirer on December 17, 1861.

between the James and York rivers. From there they would advance to Richmond. In the battles of Fair Oaks on May 31, and Seven Pines on June 1, the Confederates were driven back. In August 1862, Union troops were within twenty-five miles of Richmond when McClellan stopped to wait for reinforcements.

While McClellan waited, Confederate troops under Generals Lee and Thomas Jonathan "Stonewall" Jackson fought Union troops near Richmond. The Seven Days' Battle, from June 25 to July 1, was not won by either side. McClellan still believed he was outnumbered and ordered a retreat to the James River, ending his plan to take Richmond. President Lincoln dismissed McClellan as general in chief and replaced him with

Major General Henry Halleck. McClellan was given command of the Union forces located in the Washington, D.C., area.

At the Second Battle of Bull Run near Manassas, Virginia, on August 30, 1862, Union forces under General John Pope were defeated by Confederates under the command of Generals Lee, Jackson, and James Longstreet. Lincoln relieved Pope of his command and sent him west.

In September 1862, McClellan was again a field commander. At Antietam (Sharpsburg, Virginia), on September 17, 1862, his men stopped the Confederates. Twelve thousand Union soldiers and twelve thousand seven hundred Confederates were killed or wounded.[8] Lincoln hoped for a quick follow-up that would destroy Lee's army. He was disappointed, however, when McClellan did not cut off Lee's retreat.[9] On November 7, 1862, Lincoln replaced McClellan with Ambrose E. Burnside. The president remarked that McClellan simply had the "slows."[10]

In late 1862, under the command of General Burnside, the Army of the Potomac again advanced on Richmond. In a battle at Fredericksburg, Virginia, on December 13, Burnside's forces were badly beaten by Lee's Confederates. The Union forces were driven back to Washington, D.C. Lincoln relieved Burnside of his command.

After suffering several defeats in the West, Union forces finally gained ground. Early in 1862, troops

SOURCE DOCUMENT

A letter from William Jones, a Union soldier, written to his sister, Mary, during his tour of duty. Note the portrait of General George McClellan at the top of the soldier's stationery. Dated October 31, 1863, this letter is from the personal papers of the author. William Jones is her great-grandfather.

under the command of Ulysses S. Grant captured Fort Henry, Tennessee, on the Tennessee River. They also took Fort Donelson, Tennessee, on the Cumberland River. These two victories allowed Union forces to sweep down the Mississippi River. By June 1862, Union troops controlled most of western and eastern Tennessee and the Mississippi River south to Memphis, Tennessee.

In April 1862, the Union navy under Captain David G. Farragut forced the Confederates to surrender New Orleans, Louisiana. Additional victories strengthened the Union position along the Mississippi River. By late 1862, Vicksburg, Mississippi, was the last Confederate stronghold in the west. Grant's army attacked, but Vicksburg was heavily defended, and Union troops were stalled outside the city.

In April 1863, Grant tried again to take Vicksburg, Mississippi. In a series of attacks, he split the Confederate troops. For forty-seven days, Union forces on land and at sea fired continuously at the city. Finally, on July 4, the Confederates surrendered.

Meanwhile, General Joseph "Fighting Joe" Hooker assumed command of the Army of the Potomac in the east. Hooker's army of one hundred thirty thousand attacked Lee's sixty thousand Confederates near Fredericksburg, Virginia. Lee then withdrew his troops to Chancellorsville, Virginia, and from May 2 through May 4, 1863, the combined Lee and Jackson forces fought Hooker's men. Hooker finally retreated, but Confederate

SOURCE DOCUMENT

A general order by the President
to all Commanders of the U.S. Forces in the field.

In the progress of this war so wickedly commenced against the United States, and waged by treason and rebellion, it has become necessary to regulate our advancing arms by definite orders, of general application. In the excitement of advance, of battle, and of victory, there is danger of forgetting the dictates of justice and of christianity.

You will always remember, therefore, that this war so causelessly provoked by our enemies, is waged, on our part, solely to restore the supremacy of the Constitution, the Union, and the laws. These have been established, amidst many sacrifices of blood, treasure, and opinion, by us, by them, and especially by our common ancestry, now revered by the civilized of all nations. The work of the martyrs and patriots of the Revolution must never be overthrown by violence. We might well expect to be abandoned of Heaven, if we hesitated in the faithful and resolute defence of its best political gift to men.

It is not a war of vengeance, for that is the function alone of the Almighty. It remains for government to administer justice only under the forms of established law.

It is not a war for the subjugation of a country, for that is already an inseparable part of the United States, nor of a people, for great numbers of its inhabitants are still peaceable, loyal, and hopeful of an early deliverance, at your

A general order concerning conduct of the Civil War, sent by President Abraham Lincoln to all commanders of U.S. forces in the field, April 1, 1862.

casualties were high. Nearly one fifth of Lee's forces were killed, along with General Stonewall Jackson, who was accidentally shot by one of his own men.

In June 1863, after his victory at Chancellorsville, Lee moved his army of seventy-five thousand Confederates into southern Pennsylvania. Now under the command of General George G. Meade, the Army of the Potomac, eighty-five thousand men strong, moved to head off Lee's advance. On July 1, the two armies met at Gettysburg, Pennsylvania. The battle that followed marked a turning point in the war. The numbers of dead and wounded were heavy for both sides: twenty-three thousand Union soldiers and twenty-eight thousand Confederates.[11] Meade forced Lee to retreat but allowed him to escape to Northern Virginia. Lincoln was at first happy with Meade's victory, then angry that he had not gone after Lee.[12]

On November 19, 1863, Lincoln traveled to Pennsylvania to dedicate part of the battlefield as a cemetery. Lincoln began his Gettysburg Address with the now famous words of "Four score and seven years ago our fathers brought forth on this continent, a new nation, conceived in Liberty, and dedicated to the proposition that all men are created equal." Lincoln's short speech ended with ". . . that this nation, under God, shall have a new birth of freedom—and that government of the people, by the people, for the people, shall not perish from the earth."[13] This famous speech is one of the most inspiring in American history.

SOURCE DOCUMENT

Executive Mansion
January 8. 1863.

Ordered by the President.

Whereas on the 13th day of November, 1862, it was ordered that the Attorney General be charged with the superintendence and direction of all proceedings to be had under the Act of Congress of the 17 of July 1862 entitled "an Act to suppress insurrection, to punish treason and rebellion, and to seize and confiscate the property of rebels, and for other purposes" in so far as may concern the seizure, prosecution and condemnation of the estate, property and effects of rebels and traitors as mentioned and provided for in the fifth, sixth, and seventh sections of the said Act of Congress.

And whereas, since that time it has been ascertained that divers prosecutions have been instituted in the Courts of the United States, for the condemnation of property of rebels and traitors under the Act of Congress of August the 6th 1861, entitled "an Act to confiscate property used for insurrectionary purposes" which equally require the superintending care of the Government. Therefore

It is now further ordered by the President. That the Attorney General be charged with superintendence and direction of all proceedings to be had under the said last mentioned Act (the Act of 1861) as fully in all respects, as under the first mentioned Act (the Act of 1862)

Abraham Lincoln.

An executive order issued by Lincoln on January 8, 1863, authorizing the confiscation of "estate, property, and effects of rebels and traitors," fighting against the Union in the Civil War.

A drawing depicting Lincoln's address at the site of the Battle of Gettysburg on November 19, 1863.

Grant planned to drive the Confederate army out of Tennessee, then move on into Alabama and Georgia, but on September 19–20, Union forces were forced back to Chattanooga, Tennessee. In the Battle of Chattanooga on November 23–25, Union forces finally forced the Confederates to retreat. The Confederate army was finished in the North and was now so badly divided in the west that defeat seemed certain.

In 1864, Lincoln made Grant commander in chief of the Union army. Grant and Meade would lead the Army of the Potomac against Lee's forces in northern Virginia and push on to Richmond. Union forces under General William T. Sherman would cut off Lee's supplies in the

SOURCE DOCUMENT

Four score and seven years ago our fathers brought forth, upon this continent, a new nation, conceived in Liberty, and dedicated to the proposition that all men are created equal.

Now we are engaged in a great civil war, testing whether that nation, or any nation, so conceived, and so dedicated, can long endure. We are met here on a great battle-field of that war. We have come to dedicate a portion of it as a final resting place for those who here gave their lives that that nation might live. It is altogether fitting and proper that we should do this.

But in a larger sense we can not dedicate— we can not consecrate— we can not hallow this ground. The brave men, living and dead, who struggled here, have consecrated it far above our poor power to add or detract. The world will little note, nor long remember, what we say here, but can never forget what they did here. It is for us, the living, rather to be dedicated here to the unfinished work which they have, thus far, so nobly carried on. It is rather

One of five surviving copies of Lincoln's handwritten draft of the Gettysburg Address, delivered November 19, 1863, at the site of the Battle of Gettysburg.

Shenandoah Valley. The Army of the Potomac began its march in late March 1863.

Although both Union and Confederate forces suffered heavy casualties, Grant continued his press. "The art of war is simple enough," he said. "Find out where your enemy is, get at him as soon as you can, strike him as hard as you can and as often as you can, and keep moving on."[14] Grant's forces surrounded Petersburg, Virginia, but could not take the city. The Confederates holding Petersburg held out for another nine months.

Meanwhile, Union troops under General Philip Sheridan forced the Confederates from the Shenandoah Valley. In the summer of 1864, Sherman's ninety thousand men marched to Atlanta, Georgia. On September 1, they captured the city. On November 15, Sherman's Union troops burned Atlanta, then began their march to the sea. On their way, they destroyed everything that might help supply the Confederate army.

By April 1865, Savannah, Georgia, and Mobile, Selma, and Montgomery, Alabama, all had fallen to Union forces. The same month, Grant's army captured the railroad supplying Richmond, Virginia, and that city fell. Lee's army was prevented from joining with other Confederate forces in North Carolina.

On April 9, 1865, Robert E. Lee surrendered twenty-seven thousand eight hundred Confederate troops to Ulysses S. Grant at Appomattox Court House in southwestern Virginia. On April 18, J. E. Johnston surrendered thirty-one thousand two hundred rebels to

General Ulysses S. Grant, Commander in Chief of the Union army during the Civil War.

General Robert E. Lee, Commander in Chief of the Confederate army during the Civil War.

Sherman at Durham Station, North Carolina. The last Confederate soldiers surrendered on May 26, 1865.[15] The Civil War was over.

When the war ended, six hundred twenty thousand American men had died, and at least that many more were wounded. The North listed three hundred sixty-four thousand dead; the South listed two hundred fifty-eight thousand. About four times more men died from disease than were killed in battle. The Civil War also caused over $4 billion worth of damage to homes, crops, railroads, and the South's economy.[16]

At a terrible cost, the Union had survived. Nearly 4 million African Americans in the United States were freed from the evils of slavery. Never again would the states of the union wage war against each other to settle their differences.

8

COMMANDER IN CHIEF

While the Civil War raged, the Lincolns performed their duties as president and first lady. Robert, their oldest son, was home only during vacations from Harvard University. Three months before the Civil War ended, he was made a captain on General Grant's staff. Willie and Tad, however, roamed the house and grounds. They played soldier and rode the pony an admirer had given them.

President Lincoln's days began early and lasted late into the night. Between war-planning sessions he signed papers, spoke with members of Congress about pending laws, presided at various ceremonies, reviewed Union troops, visited battle sites, and heard the pleas of an endless parade of office seekers. While the president seemed calm in public, those close to him knew that he

Thomas "Tad" Lincoln, circa 1861, dressed in the sized-to-fit uniform of a Union officer, complete with a sword in a decorated scabbard. The Lincoln children played war games, while President Lincoln worked at winning the war.

worried constantly.[1] The numbers of war dead weighed heavily on his mind. In addition, Union defeats early in the war had lowered the president's approval rating with the American people. Criticism from congressmen who thought the war was taking too long and costing too much added to the president's burden.

Then, during the winter of 1862, both Willie and Tad Lincoln fell ill with "bilious fever." The disease was typhoid fever, probably caused by a polluted White House water system. Tad recovered, but on February 20, 1862, Willie died. Both of his parents were grief-stricken, but Mary was desolate. She did not get out of bed for three weeks and could not go to Willie's funeral or take care of Tad.

Although he, too, grieved deeply for his son, Lincoln carried on his duties as president. One important duty that could not be neglected was appointing and meeting with Cabinet members.

Lincoln chose Cabinet members who were strong political leaders. In fact, some were his political foes. Despite frequent disagreements, Lincoln overruled his Cabinet when he believed he was right. He reportedly once asked his Cabinet for advice on an important decision. A vote of Cabinet members was taken, and they all voted against Lincoln's proposed decision. He then said, "Seven nays and one aye, the ayes have it."[2]

Some of the problems Lincoln had with his Cabinet arose from the fact that some Cabinet members thought themselves superior to him.[3] This attitude resulted in

Willie, the Lincolns' twelve-year-old son, died on February 20, 1862, of "bilious fever," which was probably typhoid fever. His funeral was conducted in the East Room of the White House.

friction among Cabinet members and between the Cabinet and the president. "Cabinet officers during the Lincoln administration were known for their intrigues," says one source. "Secretary of State William H. Seward, for example, considered himself Lincoln's prime minister. Salmon P. Chase, secretary of the treasury, schemed with a few members of the Senate to remove Seward and increase his own influence."[4]

To help hold the Republican party together, Lincoln gave Cabinet positions to different factions within the party. For example, William H. Seward, secretary of state, and Edward Bates, attorney general, were former Whigs. Bates was a conservative, so to balance his Cabinet Lincoln appointed radicals Salmon P. Chase and Edwin M. Stanton as secretary of the treasury and secretary of war, respectively. Montgomery Blair, postmaster general, and Gideon Welles, secretary of the navy, were former Democrats. Lincoln rewarded political supporters in Pennsylvania by appointing Simon Cameron secretary of war. Cameron served only briefly. Similarly, Caleb B. Smith from Indiana was appointed secretary of the interior. Lincoln made few changes in his Cabinet from his first term to his second. Seward, Stanton, and Welles remained in their Cabinet posts. William Fessenden became secretary of the treasury in 1864, but his health was poor and he was replaced by Hugh McCulloch in 1865. Lincoln's second-term attorney general was James Speed, the brother of Lincoln's old friend Joshua. Secretary of the Interior

Likenesses of Lincoln appeared on many objects for sale during his presidency. The head and shoulders portrait (left) was reproduced on a cardboard cutout; the portrait on the right appeared on an orange crate.

John P. Usher replaced Caleb Smith in 1863 and served in that post during Lincoln's second term.

Although President Lincoln and members of Congress were preoccupied with war concerns, during the 1862–1863 session they managed to conduct a surprising amount of business. In May 1862, the Federal Homestead Law was passed. Under the law, anyone could have one hundred sixty acres of publicly owned land west of the Mississippi River if they claimed, occupied, and improved it for at least five years.

The Land Grant Act was passed in July 1862. The act donated some of the proceeds from public land sales to agricultural education. It led to the beginning of state university systems.

Other laws passed by the 1862–1863 Congress and signed by President Lincoln included

★ a conscription (draft) act,

★ a tax measure,

★ a protective tariff,

★ the National Banking Act, setting up a national currency and a network of national banks,

★ a bill creating the Department of Agriculture.

As the Civil War continued, Lincoln's thinking about slavery shifted. So far, the president had honored his inaugural promise not to interfere with slavery in the South. Rising antislavery feeling in the North and concern that North and South could never agree as long as slavery existed changed the president's mind.

On July 22, 1862, Lincoln told his Cabinet that he planned to issue a proclamation freeing the slaves. In the following weeks, Lincoln carefully considered all arguments for and against his proposed emancipation (freedom) proclamation. He drafted a preliminary version, and on September 22, 1862, five days after McClellan defeated Lee at Antietam, President Lincoln read his Emancipation Proclamation to his Cabinet. He then ordered that it be made public. The proclamation said that as of January 1, 1863, "all persons held as slaves within any State or designated part of a State" where people were "in rebellion against the United States shall be then, thenceforward, and forever free. . . ."[5]

In other words, the proclamation freed 4 million slaves in the Southern states that had seceded from the Union. It did not include slaves in those states that had remained in the Union.

The Emancipation Proclamation also authorized the formation of African-American Union military units. By the end of the war, one hundred eighty-six thousand African-American men had served in the Union army.[6]

The people received Lincoln's Emancipation Proclamation with mixed emotions. Antislavery citizens and slaves who heard about it were happy. Cities in the North held celebrations. The proclamation was

A painting depicting the first reading of the Emancipation Proclamation by President Lincoln.

unpopular in the South and with slave owners in the Union states and Southern border states. Jefferson Davis said it was all the more reason the Confederacy should fight on.[7] Some politicians said that it was unconstitutional. The British government criticized it because it mentioned only those slaves in the Confederacy. Many Europeans were afraid it would halt their supply of cotton.

Despite criticism, the Emancipation Proclamation went into effect. To avoid later claims that the document was unconstitutional, Lincoln proposed a thirteenth amendment to the Constitution that would ban slavery forever in the United States. On January 1, 1865, Congress approved the Thirteenth Amendment to the Constitution. The amendment was ratified by two thirds of the states on December 6, 1865.

On September 24, 1862, two days after reading the Emancipation Proclamation to his Cabinet, Lincoln again suspended the writ of habeas corpus. He had first done so soon after the attack on Fort Sumter. The suspension stated that all persons who interfered with the draft would be subject to military trial.

The military draft issue was a major concern during Lincoln's administration. The Federal Militia Act of 1862 and the Draft Act of 1863, sometimes called the Enrollment Act, allowed the federal government to require military service of all men between the ages of twenty and thirty-five and single men between thirty-five and forty-five.

SOURCE DOCUMENT

A Proclamation.

Whereas, on the twenty-second day of September, in the year of our Lord one thousand eight hundred and sixty-two, a proclamation was issued by the President of the United States, containing, among other things, the following, towit:

"That on the first day of January, in the year of our Lord one thousand eight hundred and sixty-three, all persons held as slaves within any State or designated part of a State, the people whereof shall then be in rebellion against the United States, shall be then, thenceforward, and forever free; and the Executive Government of the United States, including the military and naval authority thereof, will recognize and maintain the freedom of such persons, and will do no act or acts to repress such persons, or any of them, in any efforts they may make for their actual freedom.

"That the Executive will, on the first day of January aforesaid, by proclamation, designate the States and parts of States, if any, in which the people thereof, respectively, shall then be in rebellion against the United States; and the fact that any State, or the people thereof, shall on that day be, in good faith, represented in the Congress of the United States by members chosen thereto at elections wherein a majority of the qualified voters of such State shall have participated, shall, in the absence of strong countervailing testimony, be deemed conclusive evidence that such State, and the people thereof, are not then in rebellion against the United States."

Now, therefore I, Abraham Lincoln, President of the United States, by virtue of the power in me vested as Commander-in-Chief, of the Army and Navy of the United States, in time of actual armed rebellion against authority and government of the United States, and as a fit and necessary war measure for suppressing said rebellion, do, on this first day of January, in the year of our Lord one thousand eight hundred and sixty-three, and in accordance with my purpose so to do, publicly proclaimed for the full period of one hundred days, from the day first above mentioned, order and designate

The Emancipation Proclamation, freeing the slaves, was issued by Lincoln on January 1, 1863.

The people strongly objected to the Enrollment Act. They especially resented the fact that the act allowed a man to pay someone else to serve for him, or to pay $300 to be released from service.[8] On July 13–16, 1863, citizens in New York City rioted against this practice. One thousand were killed or wounded. The practice of paying money to avoid the draft was ended in 1864.

As the war continued, Lincoln tried to reassure the South that if the North won the war, he would not be spiteful. As early as December 8, 1863, his Proclamation of Amnesty and Reconstruction offered "full pardon with restoration of all rights of property, except as to slaves," to all rebels.[9] All Southerners who took an oath of loyalty to the Constitution and who promised to obey acts of Congress and the president regarding slavery would be given amnesty, or pardon. If 10 percent of a state's 1860 voters met these conditions, that state could write a new constitution and elect new federal congressmen and state officers.

On July 2, 1864, Congress passed the Wade-Davis bill, a harsher reconstruction measure. The bill said that all Southern states must abolish slavery and called for 50 percent, instead of 10 percent, of 1860 voters to meet conditions before reconstruction could begin. In addition, the 50 percent had to swear they had never borne arms against the Union—a difficult requirement for any Southern state to meet. Lincoln pocket-vetoed the bill. He failed to sign it within ten days after Congress adjourned, preventing it from becoming law.

SOURCE DOCUMENT

Executive Mansion,

Washington, _____ *16* _____, *1863*.

Copy.

On condition that Edward L. Hale named within, faithfully serves in his present position, until honorably discharged, he is fully pardoned for the desertion mentioned.

A. Lincoln

Nov. 16. 1863

This note written by Lincoln granted a pardon to Edward L. Hale, a soldier, on November 16, 1863.

Congressmen and others in favor of the Wade-Davis bill were angered by its defeat. President Lincoln was again denounced by those critics who disagreed with his policies.

By mid-1864, Lincoln was exhausted. He worried about squabbling among Cabinet members and among Republicans in Congress. The disapproval of the people wore him down, and the war was a constant concern. "In May 1864, while a fierce battle had raged in the Wilderness, Lincoln had scarcely slept for four nights on

Lincoln reading to Tad, from a photograph taken on February 9, 1864, by Anthony Berger. This was the first time Lincoln had posed for a photograph with a family member.

end," wrote Oscar and Lilian Handlin in *Abraham Lincoln and the Union*. "He paced his office and the War Department corridors, anxiously awaiting news from Grant's headquarters. 'I must have some relief from this terrible anxiety . . . or it will kill me.'"[10]

The 1864 presidential election was fast approaching, and Lincoln's chances for reelection seemed slim. In fact, Lincoln himself believed he would lose. "You think I don't know I am going to be beaten," he told a friend, "*but I do* and unless some great change takes place *badly beaten*."[11]

As president, Lincoln was the official nominee of the Republican party, but many Republicans did not back him. Some believed he had been too hard on the South; others said he was too soft. Some thought the Emancipation Proclamation went too far or did not go far enough. Many thought the war could have been ended quickly if the president had shown stronger leadership. Often, even Lincoln's Cabinet members were not entirely behind him. Attorney General Edward Bates said that under Lincoln the country lacked direction and "that our great want was a competent man at the head of affairs. . . ."[12]

Then in late August, Lincoln's chances for reelection improved. At the Democratic convention, the party demanded an end to the war. The Democrats then chose General George B. McClellan to run against Lincoln. (The peace platform together with a war candidate was not a winning combination.) Further improving Lincoln's

Lincoln's oldest son, Robert Todd, as a young man, taken sometime after his graduation from Harvard University in 1864. The only Lincoln son to survive past adolescence, Robert became a successful businessman. He died in 1927.

LONG ABRAHAM LINCOLN A LITTLE
LONGER.

chance for reelection was the fact that the Union forces were winning. In September, Sherman captured Atlanta, and Rear Admiral David G. Farragut captured Mobile—both major defeats for the Confederate forces.

As a result of the changing political climate, President Lincoln remained his party's candidate and was reelected in November 1864. For a brief period, the Republican party called itself the "National Union party," so Lincoln was actually a Union candidate. Andrew Johnson was elected vice-president. Lincoln and Johnson won 212 electoral votes, to McClellan's 12.[13] Southern states that had seceded were not allowed to vote.

Harper's Weekly *published this cartoon in their November 26, 1864, issue, after President Lincoln had been reelected.*

9

FATE

Wh_en Lincoln took office for the second time in March 1865, the Civil War was nearly over. On March 4, 1865, he gave his second Inaugural Address. The speech called for forgiveness and reconciliation, rather than spite and retaliation. It asked Americans, "With malice toward none," to "strive on to finish the work we are in; to bind up the nation's wounds; to care for him who shall have borne the battle, and for his widow, and his orphan—to do all which may achieve and cherish a just and lasting peace among ourselves, and with all nations."[1]

On April 9, 1865, Lee surrendered to Grant. The terms of surrender were generous. Grant allowed rebel soldiers to keep their horses and mules and said they were free to go home. As long as they swore to be loyal to the Union and never again threatened war, they would not be punished by the government. The seceded states soon realized that under Lincoln's plans for reconstruction, they would not be treated as enemies but would be welcomed back into the Union.

At about the same time that Lee surrendered to Grant, a young actor was hatching a dark plot that would change the course of history.

John Wilkes Booth, a twenty-six-year-old actor from Baltimore, Maryland, did not fight in the Civil War, although he supported the South. He had grown up on a farm in Maryland that was worked by slaves, so unlike President Lincoln, he was proslavery. Booth feared for the South's future under President Lincoln. In fact, he told his brother Edwin that he feared Lincoln would be made "King of America."[2]

At least a year before the war ended, Booth persuaded a few friends to help him kidnap the president. They would take Lincoln to Richmond, Virginia, and hold him until the North agreed to release all Confederate prisoners. Booth and his group spent months plotting, but the war ended before they were ready to act.

Booth's plan changed, probably soon after the war ended. Instead of kidnapping the president, Booth would retaliate for the South's defeat by killing him.

On Good Friday, April 14, 1865, the Lincolns decided to attend a performance of *Our American Cousin* at Ford's Theatre on 10th Street in Washington. They asked several friends to go with them, but only two accepted: twenty-eight-year-old Major Henry R. Rathbone and his fiancée, twenty-year-old Clara H. Harris, the daughter of New York Senator Ira Harris.

The Lincolns and their guests arrived at the theater about 8:30 P.M., after the play had begun. Once inside the theater, they took their seats in the presidential box. The box had been decorated for the president's visit. American flags hung at the sides of the box and were draped over the rail. A portrait of George Washington hung between the flags on the rail. A red rocking chair had been brought from the theater owner's home for Lincoln's comfort. Comfortable chairs and a sofa were provided for the first lady and guests.

Earlier in the day John Wilkes Booth had secretly visited the theater box where the presidential party would sit. He had made a hole in the plaster near the box's door on the inside, so that a small board could be wedged against the door. This would prevent anyone from opening the door after Booth entered the box.

While the president's party enjoyed the play, Booth put his plan into action. Shortly after 10 P.M., he walked up the stairs to the closed door of the president's box. Charles Forbes, the president's footman and messenger, sat near the door.[3] Booth showed a personal calling card and Forbes allowed him to enter, probably thinking that the well-known actor wanted to pay his respects to the president.

Once inside the presidential box, Booth closed the

door, inserting the wedge he had earlier hidden. The audience was laughing at the action on stage, and no one in the box heard Booth enter. He pulled a .44-caliber, single-shot derringer from his pocket, then stepped up behind the president and fired at the back of his head. The bullet entered behind Lincoln's left ear, cut a furrow into his brain, and lodged behind his right eye. Lincoln's head slumped forward on his chest. Mrs. Lincoln reached to support her husband, perhaps thinking that he had fallen asleep.

Major Henry Rathbone realized that a shot had been fired and lunged at Booth. Booth dropped his pistol, drew a knife, and slashed Rathbone's left arm to the bone. The wounded Rathbone could not hold onto Booth, and the assassin climbed onto the railing of the box and jumped some twelve feet to the stage below.

As he jumped, Booth's spur caught on the flags draped over the box railing, causing him to land off balance. The impact broke a bone in his lower left leg, but he was able to limp away before the shocked actors and spectators realized what had happened. Some believe that Booth broke his leg later in a fall from his horse. *"Sic semper tyrannis!"* ("Thus always to tyrants") he shouted as he made his escape.[4]

Only when they heard Mrs. Lincoln's screams and Major Rathbone's shouts did the crowd of one thousand realize that something was terribly wrong. In the meantime, Booth had run out the back door of the theater into the alley. His horse was waiting for him, held by a stagehand named Peanut John, who knew Booth but was not in on the plan. Booth hit Peanut John once with his gun, then kicked him, perhaps to keep him from telling any pursuers in which direction he was heading when he escaped. Booth then mounted his horse and rode away into the night.

Inside the theater, women screamed, men shouted and cursed, and people cried. Two physicians, Charles A. Leale and Charles Sabin Taft, were in the audience that evening and were among the first to reach the president after the shooting. They found a weak pulse, but knew the wound was fatal. The president would never survive a jarring carriage ride to the White House, six blocks away, so several men carried him outside, into the street.

Lincoln's bearers were told to bring the wounded president inside a rooming house located across the street from the theater. They brought the unconscious president to a room with an empty bed and laid him down.

Lincoln's inner circle soon learned the full extent of Booth's plot. When Cabinet members Edwin Stanton and Gideon Welles arrived at the rooming house, they said that Secretary of State William Seward had also been attacked. On April 5, Seward had been injured in a carriage accident. On the night of April 14, he was still bedridden, recovering from a broken jaw and a broken right arm. At nearly the same time that Lincoln was shot, a man later named as Lewis Thornton Powell, also

The actor, John Wilkes Booth, was Lincoln's assassin. The date of this photograph is unknown.

known as Lewis Paine, entered Seward's home. A servant let him into the house when he claimed to have medicine from Seward's doctor. He forced his way into Seward's room, wounding a male nurse named George F. Robinson and Seward's two sons, Frederick and Augustus, in the process. Frederick was pistol-whipped until he became unconscious and Augustus Seward and Robinson were stabbed.

Paine knifed Secretary Seward, deeply cutting the side of his face. Seward's life was saved only by the metal cage his doctor had placed over his face, to hold his jaw in place while it healed. Augustus Seward would recall later that the assailant cried over and over, "I'm mad! I'm mad!"[5]

Paine escaped on his horse but was later captured. All of the men he attacked survived.

It was later learned that Vice-President Andrew Johnson had also been marked for death that night. George Atzerodt, a friend of Booth's who was to have done the deed, backed out at the last minute.

Throughout the night of April 15, Lincoln lay dying. Some ninety people, including physicians, congressmen, and Cabinet members, passed through the tiny room. Mary Lincoln was frantic with grief. When President Lincoln died at 7:22 A.M., she was resting in another room.

Secretary of War Stanton immediately organized a search for the president's murderer, who had been identified as John Wilkes Booth. Detectives learned that at about 10:45 P.M. a man on a horse had been stopped by military guards at the Navy Yard Bridge. The rider gave his name as Booth and said he was on his way home to southern Maryland after completing errands in Washington. The guards let him pass. Later this information would help Booth's trackers find him.

A man named David Herold was also allowed to cross the bridge that night. Unknown to the guards, Herold was one of Booth's accomplices and was riding to catch up with him.

Booth was in great pain from his broken leg, and he and Herold rode to the house of Dr. Samuel Mudd near Bryantown, Maryland. Booth had previously met Mudd, but the doctor claimed later that the two men gave false names and had disguised themselves, so that he did not recognize them. Dr. Mudd splinted Booth's broken leg and went back to bed.

About 5:00 P.M. on April 15, Booth and Herold left Mudd's house and hid for several days in various locations. By April 26, the fugitives finally reached the farm of Richard H. Garrett, where they were allowed to sleep in a tobacco barn. The Union cavalry had picked up the trail of the two men, and in the early morning hours soldiers surrounded the barn. Herold surrendered, but Booth had vowed he would never be taken alive. The soldiers set fire to the barn to smoke him out, but a man named Boston Corbett, acting against orders, shot and killed the actor.

Authorities learned that Booth and his group had

held their meetings at Mary Surratt's boardinghouse in Washington, D.C. Louis Weichmann, a boarder at the Surratt house, claimed to know nothing about the plot but gave detectives the names of those who had frequently met with Booth.

In the days after the assassination, wild rumors spread. One story was that Booth had acted on the orders of Jefferson Davis, Robert E. Lee, and other Southern leaders who had planned the president's murder in retaliation for the South's defeat. Investigators could find no evidence, however, that these stories were true. Jefferson Davis, former president of the Confederacy, was imprisoned briefly. He was eventually released when he could not be connected to the plot.

By the end of April, eight accused conspirators had been arrested. Their trial began on May 9 and on June 30, 1865, all eight were found guilty. Mary E. Surratt, Lewis Thornton Powell, George A. Atzerodt, and David E. Herold were sentenced to hang, and the executions were carried out on July 7, 1865.

Mary Surratt's son, John, fled the country when the search for Lincoln's assassins began. He was finally arrested in Egypt and returned to the United States. He was tried on June 10, 1867, for conspiring to kill President Lincoln. The jury could not agree on a verdict, and the case was dismissed.

Samuel Arnold and Michael O'Laughlin had been in on the original kidnapping plot, but they may not have known that Booth planned to kill the president.

Nevertheless, Arnold, O'Laughlin, and Dr. Samuel Mudd all received life sentences. George Spangler, a theater handyman who helped Booth get into and out of the theater, got six years.[6] O'Laughlin died of yellow fever while in prison. In February 1869, President Andrew Johnson ordered that Spangler, Arnold, and Mudd be freed.

While Booth and Herold were still running from the authorities, a sorrowful nation paid tribute to its fallen president. On April 18, twenty-five thousand people filed sadly through the White House, where Lincoln's body lay in state. Funeral services were held in the East Room on April 19.

A drawing depicting Lincoln's funeral procession as it passed through Washington, D.C. The hearse containing the president's coffin, pulled by six white horses, is seen in the foreground. The drawing first appeared in the May 6, 1865, issue of Harper's Weekly *magazine.*

On April 21, Lincoln's body and the body of his son Willie were placed on a special train, to be taken home to Springfield, Illinois, for burial. Willie had previously been buried in Washington, D.C., but his body was removed from its grave to be taken home with his father. The train retraced the president's inaugural journey of 1861, this time to allow the people to say good-bye. In each city along the way, ceremonies were held and people viewed the president's body.

On May 4, 1865, Abraham Lincoln was finally laid to rest in Oak Ridge Cemetery in Springfield, next to his sons Eddie and Willie. In 1901, the bodies were placed in a permanent monument.

The upper portion of the Lincoln Memorial statue designed by Daniel Chester French in 1922. Thirty-six Doric columns, one for each state that existed when Lincoln died, support the roof of the memorial.

10

LINCOLN'S LEGACY

F rom the beginning of his presidency, Lincoln made it clear that he would follow the United States Constitution. He would also work to preserve the Union of states, against all threats to disband it. When the Civil War began, he saw it as his duty to use the power of the federal government to crush the revolt.

As Commander in Chief, Lincoln used the emergency powers of the presidency as no president had done before him. Shortly after his election in 1861, he increased the size of the armed forces and authorized the money to pay for supplies and troops—all before Congress was in session.

Later, when he suspended the writ of habeas corpus, he was widely criticized. Many historians, however, see

Lincoln's act as strengthening the presidency. For example, presidential scholar Clinton Rossiter wrote: "The one great precedent is what Lincoln did. . . . Future presidents will know where to look for historical support. . . . The law of the Constitution, as it actually exists, must be considered to read that in a condition of martial necessity the president has the power to suspend the privilege of the writ of habeas corpus."[1]

Lincoln believed that the war between the states could not be resolved without freeing the slaves, and he considered their emancipation well within his powers as president. Although the Emancipation Proclamation was unpopular with many groups, it led to the Thirteenth Amendment to the United States Constitution, which banned slavery in America forever.

Once the Civil War had been won by the North, Lincoln did not want the seceded states to be unduly punished for their role. He was firm in putting down the rebellion, but he was equally firm in his resolve that coming back into the Union should be made as painless as possible for the seceded states. As he stated in his second Inaugural Address, the "nation's wounds" should be healed "With malice toward none, with charity for all. . . ."[2] It was a national tragedy that he did not live to see his plans for reconstruction put into action.

While Americans paid a terrible price for the Civil War, some important issues were settled:

> ★ The Union is permanent and cannot be dissolved at will.

★ The United States Constitution is the highest law of the land.

★ Slavery was abolished in the United States, freeing nearly 4 million African Americans.

★ States must air grievances through legislative channels, rather than through secession or acts of war.

★ The executive branch of government has broad emergency powers when the country is at war.

Throughout his term as president, Lincoln's message to the people was the same: Everyone deserved the same fair chance to succeed in life, and this right should be protected for future generations. During the Civil War, he expressed this belief to the 166th Ohio Regiment:

> It is not merely for today, but for all time to come that we should perpetuate for our children's children this great and free government, which we have enjoyed all our lives. I beg you to remember this, not merely for my sake, but for yours. I happen temporarily to occupy this big White House. I am a living witness that any one of your children may look to come here as my father's child has. It is in order that each of you may have through this free government which we have enjoyed, an open field and a fair chance for your industry, enterprise, and intelligence; that you may all have equal privileges in the race of life, with all its desirable human aspirations. It is for this the struggle should be maintained. . . . The nation is worth fighting for. . . .[3]

Although Abraham Lincoln has become a folk hero, many of his strongest traits have been documented as

A formal portrait of Lincoln, taken by Brady & Co., photographers, a few months before his death in 1865.

fact. Those who knew him well spoke of his sense of humor, his love for storytelling, his talent for public speaking and persuasion, his unique political skills, his patience, and his kind nature. He suffered from severe depression all of his life. Despite this disadvantage, he made the difficult decisions required of an American president in the nation's most troubled times.

Lincoln came from humble beginnings to assume the nation's highest office. As he matured, he became an expert campaign organizer and politician, and he used his "common man" image to his political advantage.

Many historians claim that Abraham Lincoln strengthened the office of president for those who came after him. He also dignified the office, bringing to it the same honesty, talent for negotiation, and fair-minded principles that marked all the fifty-six years of his life.

Chronology

1809—Feb. 12: Born in Hardin County, Kentucky.

1816—Lincoln family moves to Indiana.

1818—Mother, Nancy Hanks Lincoln, dies.

1819—Father, Thomas Lincoln, marries Sarah Bush Johnston.

1834—Runs for state legislature and wins.

1837—March 1: Obtains license to practice law.

April 15: Moves from New Salem to Springfield, Illinois.

1838—Reelected to the Illinois General Assembly.

1840—Engaged to Mary Todd.

1841—Jan. 1: Breaks engagement to Mary Todd.

1842—Nov. 4: Marries Mary Todd.

1843—Aug.1: Son Robert Lincoln born.

1844—Forms partnership with William H. Herndon.

1846—March 10: Son Edward Baker Lincoln born.

1847—Elected to United States House of Representatives.

1850—Feb. 1: Son Edward Baker Lincoln, age three years, ten months, dies.

1850—Dec. 21: Son William Wallace "Willie" Lincoln born.

1853—April 4: Son Thomas "Tad" Lincoln born.

1856—Helps organize Republican party in Illinois.

1858—Lincoln-Douglas debates; loses Senate race to Douglas.

1860—November 6: Elected to first term as president of the United States.

1860 —December–March: Seven states leave the
–1861   Union.

1861—April 14: Confederates capture Fort Sumter.

1862—Jan. 27: Issues General War Order No. 1.

Feb. 20: Son William Wallace Lincoln dies at age twelve.

May 20: Signs Federal Homestead Law.

July 7: Land Grant Act approved.

September 17: McClellan defeats Robert E. Lee at Antietam.

September 24: Lincoln suspends writ of habeas corpus.

1863—January 1: Issues Emancipation Proclamation.

November 19: Gives Gettysburg Address.

1864—September; General Sherman's Union forces march through Georgia.

November: President Lincoln reelected.

1865—January 1: Congress approves Thirteenth Amendment to the Constitution, abolishing slavery in the United States. (Amendment ratified on December 6, 1865.)

March 4: Gives second Inaugural Address.

April 9: General Robert E. Lee surrenders Confederate troops to General Ulysses S. Grant at Appomattox Court House, Virginia.

April 14: President Lincoln shot by John Wilkes Booth in Ford's Theatre, Washington, D.C.

April 15: Lincoln dies at age fifty-six.

April 26: John Wilkes Booth shot to death.

May 4: Lincoln buried at Oak Ridge Cemetery, Springfield, Illinois.

Chapter Notes

Chapter 1. Sneaking Into Washington

1. Ida M. Tarbell, *The Life of Abraham Lincoln: Volume One* (New York: Macmillan Company, 1928), p. 450.

2. William Gutman, *Andrew Jackson and the New Populism* (New York: Barron's Educational Series, Inc., 1987), p. 151.

3. Philip B. Kunhardt, Jr., Philip B. Kunhardt III, and Peter W. Kunhardt, *Lincoln: An Illustrated Biography* (New York: Alfred A. Knopf, 1992), p. 4.

4. "Davis, Jefferson," Microsoft Encarta 96 Encyclopedia, 1993–1995. Microsoft Corporation, Funk & Wagnalls Corporation.

5. Kunhardt, Kunhardt, and Kunhardt, p. 16.

6. David Herbert Donald, *Lincoln* (New York: Simon and Schuster, 1995), p. 279.

7. Ibid.

8. Mark E. Neely, Jr., *Abraham Lincoln and the Promise of America: The Last Hope of Earth* (Cambridge, Mass.: Harvard University Press, 1993), p. 184.

9. Emanuel Hertz, *The Hidden Lincoln: From the Letters and Papers of William H. Herndon* (New York: The Viking Press, 1938), p. 5.

Chapter 2. Born in a Log Cabin

1. Michael Burlingame, *The Inner World of Abraham Lincoln* (Urbana and Chicago: University of Illinois Press, 1994), p. 21.

2. Ibid., p. 37.

3. David Herbert Donald, *Lincoln* (London: Jonathan Cape, 1995), p. 31.

4. Mark E. Neely, Jr., *Abraham Lincoln and the Promise of America: The Last Best Hope of Earth* (Cambridge, Mass.: Harvard University Press, 1993), p. 5.

5. Ibid.

6. Philip B. Kunhardt, Jr., Philip B. Kunhardt III, and Peter W. Kunhardt, *Lincoln: An Illustrated Biography* (New York: Alfred A. Knopf, 1992), p. 39.

7. Mark E. Neely, Jr., *The Abraham Lincoln Encyclopedia* (New York: McGraw-Hill Book Company, 1982), p. 188.

8. Burlingame, pp. 37–39.

Chapter 3. Political Ambitions

1. Philip B. Kunhardt, Jr., Philip B. Kunhardt III, and Peter W. Kunhardt, *Lincoln: An Illustrated Biography* (New York: Alfred A. Knopf, 1992), p. 45.

2. Ibid.

3. Oscar Handlin and Lilian Handlin, *Abraham Lincoln and the Union* (Boston: Little, Brown and Company, 1980), p. 23.

4. Mark E. Neely, Jr., *Abraham Lincoln and the Promise of America: The Last Best Hope of Earth* (Cambridge, Mass.: Harvard University Press, 1993), p. 8.

5. Ida M. Tarbell, *The Life of Abraham Lincoln: Volume One* (New York: Macmillan, 1928), p. 121.

6. Ibid., p. 151.

Chapter 4. The Law and Politics

1. Oscar Handlin and Lilian Handlin, *Abraham Lincoln and the Union* (Boston: Little, Brown and Company, 1980), p. 34.

2. David Herbert Donald, *Lincoln* (London: Jonathan Cape, 1995), p. 64.

3. Carl Sandburg, *Abraham Lincoln: The Prairie Years* (New York: Harcourt, Brace & Company, Inc., 1926), p. 215.

4. Donald, p. 66.

5. Sandburg, p. 200.

6. Ibid., pp. 205–206.

7. Mark E. Neely, Jr., *The Abraham Lincoln Encyclopedia* (New York: McGraw-Hill Book Company, 1982), p. 193.

8. Donald, p. 82.

9. Sandburg, p. 212.

10. Neely, *The Abraham Lincoln Encyclopedia*, p. 198.

Chapter 5. Family and Politics

1. *Abraham Lincoln: Speeches and Writings 1832–1858* (New York: Literary Classics of the United States, 1989), p. 20.

2. Ibid.

3. David Herbert Donald, *Lincoln* (London: Jonathan Cape, 1995), p. 87.

4. Michael Burlingame, *The Inner World of Abraham Lincoln* (Urbana and Chicago: University of Illinois Press, 1994), pp. 93–94.

5. Justin G. Turner and Linda Levitt Turner, *Mary Todd Lincoln: Her Life and Letters* (New York: Alfred A. Knopf, 1972), p. 24.

6. Ibid., p. 30.

7. Ibid., p. 31.

8. Donald, p. 100.

9. Mark E. Neely, Jr., *Abraham Lincoln and the Promise of America: The Last Best Hope of Earth* (Cambridge, Mass.: Harvard University Press, 1993), p. 33.

10. Stephen B. Oates, *Abraham Lincoln: The Man Behind the Myths* (New York: Harper & Row, 1984), p. 62.

11. Donald, p. 139.

12. Ibid., p. 140.

Chapter 6. Victory and Conflict

1. David Herbert Donald, *Lincoln* (London: Jonathan Cape, 1995), p. 168.

2. "Kansas-Nebraska Act," Microsoft Encarta 96 Encyclopedia, 1993–1995. Microsoft Corporation, Funk & Wagnalls Corporation.

3. Ibid.

4. *Abraham Lincoln: Speeches and Writings 1832–1858* (New York: Literary Classics of the United States, 1989), p. 315.

5. Donald, pp. 193–194.

6. Philip B. Kunhardt, Jr., Philip B. Kunhardt III, and Peter W. Kunhardt, *Lincoln: An Illustrated Biography* (New York: Alfred A. Knopf, 1992), p. 106.

7. "Dred Scott Case," Microsoft Encarta 96 Encyclopedia, 1993–1995. Microsoft Corporation, Funk & Wagnalls Corporation.

8. *Abraham Lincoln: Speeches and Writings 1832–1858*, p. 426.

9. Stephen B. Oates, *Abraham Lincoln: The Man Behind the Myths* (New York: Harper & Row, 1984), p. 76.

10. Harold Holzer, ed. *The Lincoln-Douglas Debates: The First Complete, Unexpurgated Text* (New York: HarperCollins, 1993), p. 27.

11. Oates, p. 77.

12. "Brown, John," Microsoft Encarta 96 Encyclopedia, 1993–1995. Microsoft Corporation, Funk & Wagnalls Corporation.

13. Kunhardt, Kunhardt, and Kunhardt p. 111.

14. Donald, p. 239.

15. Holzer, p. 28.

16. Mark E. Neely, Jr., *The Abraham Lincoln Encyclopedia* (New York: McGraw-Hill Book Company, 1982), p. 99.

Chapter 7. A House Divided

1. *The World Almanac and Book of Facts 1996* (Mahwah, N.J.: World Almanac Books, 1996), p. 523.

2. Lincoln's First Inaugural Address. "Works of Abraham Lincoln," Liberty Online Home Page, & Copy 1995, Procyon Publishing.

3. Ibid.

4. Leon F. Litwack, "Civil War, American," Microsoft Encarta 96 Encyclopedia, 1993–1995. Microsoft Corporation, Funk & Wagnalls Corporation.

5. Philip B. Kunhardt, Jr., Philip B. Kunhardt III, and Peter W. Kunhardt, *Lincoln: An Illustrated Biography* (New York: Alfred A. Knopf, 1992), p. 154.

6. Mark E. Neely, Jr., *The Abraham Lincoln Encyclopedia* (New York: McGraw-Hill Book Company, 1982), p. 200.

7. Ibid.

8. Litwack, "Civil War, American."

9. Ibid.

10. Neely, *The Abraham Lincoln Encyclopedia*, p. 201.

11. Kunhardt, Kunhardt, and Kunhardt, p. 215.

12. David Herbert Donald, *Lincoln* (London: Jonathan Cape, 1995), pp. 446–447.

13. "Two Versions of the Gettysburg Address," The World Book Multimedia Encyclopedia™ (World Book, Inc., 1996.), Windows version 3.2.

14. "Grant, Ulysses S.," Microsoft Encarta 96 Encyclopedia, 1993–1995.

15. The World Almanac and Book of Facts 1996, Microsoft Corporation, Funk & Wagnalls Corporation. p. 500.

16. Litwack, "Civil War, American."

Chapter 8. Commander in Chief

1. David Herbert Donald, *Lincoln* (London: Jonathan Cape, 1995), p. 358.

2. W. Craig Bledsoe, Harrison Donnelly, Richard A. Karno, Stephen L. Robertson, and Margaret C. Thompson, *Cabinets and Counselors: The President and the Executive Branch* (Washington, D.C.: Congressional Quarterly, Inc., 1989), p. 59.

3. Ibid.

4. Ibid.

5. "The Emancipation Proclamation," prepared by Gerald Murphy, The Cleveland Free-Net-aa300, distributed by the Cybercasting Services Division of the National Public Telecomputing Network (NPTN), 1996.

6. "Civil War, American," Microsoft Encarta 96 Encyclopedia, 1993–1995. Microsoft Corporation, Funk & Wagnalls Corporation.

7. Donald, p. 378.

8. "Conscription," Microsoft Encarta 96 Encyclopedia, 1993–1995. Microsoft Corporation, Funk & Wagnalls Corporation.

9. Donald, p. 471.

10. Oscar Handlin and Lilian Handlin, *Abraham Lincoln and the Union* (Boston: Little, Brown and Company, 1980), p. 165.

11. Donald, p. 529.

12. Ibid., p. 528.

13. "Presidential Elections, 1789 to 1992," *1995 Information Please Almanac* (New York: Houghton Mifflin Company, 1995), p. 640.

Chapter 9. Fate

1. "Lincoln's Second Inaugural Address," "Works of Abraham Lincoln," Liberty Online Home Page & Copy 1995, Procyon Publishing.

2. Mark E. Neely, Jr., *The Abraham Lincoln Encyclopedia* (New York: McGraw-Hill Book Company, 1982), p. 34.

3. David Herbert Donald, *Lincoln* (London: Jonathon Cape, 1993), p. 597.

4. Champ Clark, and the editors of Time-Life Books, "The Assassination: Death of the President," *The Civil War* (Alexandria: Time-Life Books, 1987), p. 85.

5. Ibid., p. 96.

6. Lloyd Lewis, *The Assassination of Lincoln: History and Myth* (Lincoln: University of Nebraska Press, 1994), pp. 197–198.

Chapter 10. Lincoln's Legacy

1. Harold F. Bass, Jr., W. Craig Bledsoe, Christopher J. Bosso, Daniel C. Diller, Dean J. Peterson, and James Brian Watts, *Powers of the Presidency* (Washington, D.C.: Congressional Quarterly, Inc., 1989), p. 172.

2. "Lincoln's Second Inaugural Address," "Works of Abraham Lincoln," Liberty Online Home Page & Copy 1995, Procyon Publishing.

3. Donald T. Phillips, *Lincoln on Leadership: Executive Strategies for Tough Times* (New York: Warner Books, 1992), pp. 164–165.

Further Reading

Donald, David Herbert. *Lincoln*. New York: Simon & Schuster, 1995.

Freedman, Russell. *Lincoln: A Photobiography*. New York: Clarion Books, 1987.

Kunhardt, Edith. *Honest Abe*. New York: Greenwillow Books, 1993.

Kunhardt, Philip B., Jr., Philip B. Kunhardt III, and Peter W. Kunhardt. *Lincoln: An Illustrated Biography*. New York: Alfred A. Knopf, 1992.

Lincoln, Abraham. *The Collected Poetry of Abraham Lincoln*. Springfield, Illinois: 1971.

———. *The Gettysburg Address*. Boston: Houghton Mifflin, 1995.

Reef, Catherine. *The Lincoln Memorial*. New York: Dillon Press, 1994.

Wills, Garry. *Lincoln at Gettysburg: The Words That Remade America*. New York: Simon & Schuster, 1992.

Places to Visit

Kentucky

Abraham Lincoln Birthplace National Historic Site, Hodgenville, (502) 358-3874. Located on the site Sinking Spring Farm, where Lincoln was born. An original log cabin from the nineteenth century has been reconstructed inside. Open year-round except Christmas.

Lincoln's Boyhood Home, Hodgenville, (502) 549-3741. Site of the Knob Creek farm where Lincoln lived from age two to seven. A replica of the family log cabin contains historic items and antiques. Open April-November.

Illinois

Lincoln's New Salem State Park, 20 miles NW of Springfield on State Route 97, (217) 632-7953. Reconstructed log cabin village where Lincoln spent his early adult years. Features twenty-three timber buildings, including a sawmill and gristmill, the Rutledge tavern, the Lincoln-Berry store and a stagecoach stop. Open year-round except Thanksgiving, Christmas, New Year's Day.

Lincoln Home National Historic Site, 8th and Jackson, Springfield, (217) 492-4150. The only home Lincoln ever owned. Closed: Thanksgiving, Christmas, New Year's Day.

Lincoln-Herndon Law Offices, 6th and Adams, Springfield, (217) 782-4836. The only surviving building in which Lincoln kept working law offices. Closed same as above.

Old State Capitol, 5th and Adams, Springfield, (217) 282-4836. The center of government in Illinois from 1839-1876.

Restored and furnished as it was during Lincoln's legislative years. Closed same as above.

Lincoln's Tomb State Historic Site, Oak Ridge Cemetery, Springfield, (217) 782-2717. Closed same as above.

For more information about these and other Springfield sites, write: Springfield Visitors Bureau, 624 E. Adams, Springfield, IL 62701. Phone: (217) 789-2360. Or: 1-800-545-7300.

Indiana

Lincoln Boyhood National Memorial and adjacent *Lincoln State Park*, four miles W of Santa Claus on State Route 162, (812) 937-4757. Site of the farm where Lincoln grew up. Includes a reconstructed log cabin, the graves of his mother and sister, a school, a working farmstead, and the Lincoln family church. Closed same as above.

For information about the Lincoln Heritage Trail, which includes historic sites in Kentucky, Indiana, and Illinois, write: Lincoln Heritage Trail Foundation, 702 Bloomington Road, Champaign, IL 61820.

Pennsylvania

Gettysburg National Military Park, Gettysburg, (717) 334-1124. Site of the bloodiest battle in American history and of Lincoln's most famous speech. Closed same as above.

Washington, D.C.

Ford's Theatre National Historic Site, 511 10th Street, N.W., (202) 426-6924. Restored to its original appearance, it includes a basement museum containing many objects associated with Lincoln's life and career. During the theatrical season, it is closed for afternoon matinees and rehearsals on Thursdays, Saturdays, and Sundays. Across the street, at number 516, is *Petersen House*, where Lincoln died on April 15. Closed Christmas.

Internet Addresses

History, Anecdotes, Quizzes and More About President Lincoln

http://www.yahooligans.com/Around_the_World/
History/People/U_S_Presidents/Abraham_Lincoln

History: People: Presidents: Lincoln, Abraham

http://msn.yahoo.com/msn/Arts/Humanities/
History/U_S_History/People/Presidents/
Lincoln_Abraham_1809_1865_

Poems of Abraham Lincoln

http://www.awb.com/abepoems.html

White House History and Tours

http://www.whitehouse.gov/WH/glimpse/
presidents/html/al16.html

Index